\Brew·er\, n.
   (1) One who brews; one whose occupation is to prepare malt liquors or hot beverages such as coffee. **Source** *Webster's Revised Unabridged Dictionary*
   (2) One that stirs things up or causes trouble. In action to be imminent; impending: "storms brewing on every frontier"
   (3) The name of the trouble-making coffee drinker that authored this book

Sip carefully and enjoy!

Table of Contents

Fresh From The Brewer

Fresh From The Brewer

Sips Of Wisdom From The Carpenter's Cup

Troy Brewer

cP

Aventine Press

Published by Aventine Press
1023 4th Ave #204
San Diego CA, 92101
www.aventinepress.com

ISBN: 1-59330-246-0

Printed in the United States of America

INTRODUCTION

God loves coffee. Though I cannot find a scripture for it, I am sure that addiction to coffee is not spiritually considered addiction any more than addiction to water is sin. It's just the way God made things.

God, in His incredible providence, could have named His people anything, but as a testimony to His personal love of coffee, He called them "*HE-BREWS*". (*dash added by the author*)

I've heard it called such vulgar terms as "beanwater" and "Joe", but such is the day we live in. This is the same crowd that would say, "Jesus is my homeboy" and beg God to bless their tattoos.

I have witnessed the horror of multi-million dollar lawsuits from trial lawyers and gullible old ladies demanding that it be served "luke warm" and not hot from the percolator. No doubt Jesus Himself saw this day coming and prophesied of it in Revelation saying:

So then because thou art lukewarm, and neither cold nor hot, I will spue thee out of my mouth. **Rev 3:16 KJV**

Not me! I know when things are sacred and when it is time to be respectful, so I considered drinking that wonderful cup of dark blessing to be the perfect metaphor for slowly sipping on the revelation that God gives us.

Of course my name does come into play here. My last name really is Brewer and about a year ago we had the privilege of getting my weekly E-mails published in some local newspapers. I thought "Fresh from the Brewer' would be kind of catchy and it's something that has worked well for us since then.

What you are about to read is a collection of these columns on various subjects, from different times of this past year. In some ways it reads like a journal and there are a lot of personal recollections in it. I think this is appropriate because we are on a journey together and it is very personal how Jesus shows us things and patiently teaches us.

Don't let that keep you from letting the Lord show you some powerful things to "sip" or meditate on. I was using those personal encounters in ministry to simply say, "The kingdom of God is just like that!"

You can read this book all the way through or use it as a devotional. Either way, I hope that it is more than just something for your coffee table.

Blessings on you and the cup that you drink from.

Troy A. Brewer
Joshua, Texas

MORE THAN A BROKEN RECORD

Now Moses kept the flock of Jethro his father-in-law, the priest of Midian: and he led the flock to the backside of the desert, and came to the mountain of God, even to Horeb.
And the angel of the LORD appeared unto him in a flame of fire out of the midst of a bush: and he looked, and, behold, the bush burned with fire, and the bush was not consumed.
And Moses said, I will now turn aside, and see this great sight, why the bush is not burnt. And when the LORD saw that he turned aside to see, God called unto him out of the midst of the bush, and said, Moses, Moses. And he said, Here am I.
And he said, Draw not nigh hither: put off thy shoes from off thy feet, for the place whereon thou standest is holy ground.
Exodus 3:1-5

A couple of funny things happened when Moses met the Lord on that incredible day. The first being that, it seems like God kind of stuttered when He called him. He didn't just say "Hey, Moses!" No he said "Moses, Moses". I want to get to that a little later, but first let me point out the 2nd strange thing that God did. He had Moses take off his shoes.

For the record, there is a good possibility that God would not have made that request had it been my little boy Luke there instead of Moses. Luke has the incredible gift of stinking up an entire house when he takes off only one of his shoes. He is rather famous in the north part of Johnson County and in the places where we do our missions trips. Oh, he's a great kid, but the smell that comes from his shoes has been known to give people instant headaches, including his loving dad.

Last week we were in central Mexico at an orphanage. I was there with a whole bunch of teenagers and there were no bathroom facilities. We went a week without taking a shower. That was ok with all of us until little Luke took off his shoes in the room where most of us were sleeping. The funk was such that he had to sleep in his drawers with his shoes on. It's a strange thing to me that God would have Moses take off his shoes. While I was watching Luke sleep, I was thinking about that very thing.

The thing I want to focus on is the fact that God kind of stuttered when He first called on the man that would deliver an entire nation. Though some would argue that Moses had a speech impediment, God never did. There is a reason for everything God does, even if we are not smart enough to have a clue about any of His intentions. When God calls somebody's name twice, it is very intentional and it means that the next thing He is going to say is "Stop what you are doing and get with My program." It means that He is changing things altogether in the one He is speaking to.

You can see this when the Lord stopped Abraham from killing Isaac in Genesis 22. You find it again when the Lord was encouraging Jacob to go ahead and travel to Egypt in Genesis 46. Another excellent example is when Jesus confronts Martha about her priorities in Luke 10:41. "Martha, Martha…", He said. And of course the most famous example of this is when brother Saul got knocked of his physical and proverbial "high horse" in Acts chapter 9.

"SAUL, SAUL WHY DO YOU PERSECUTE ME?"

No, it's not that Jesus was stuttering, it's that He was using God's kind of lingo to say "stop what you are doing and get with My program. He doesn't mind repeating himself. It's a blessing when the Lord does that. The worst thing that could ever happen to you and me is for God to take His hand off of us and just let us go our own natural course.

We did not come equipped with a neutral in our spiritual gearbox. When we get out from under the hand of God, we start sliding backwards and gaining momentum into things that destroy us. This is why it is such a blessing for God to intervene and tell us to stop what we are doing and get with His program.

Maybe God sounds like a broken record to you. May be the Lord keeps saying the same thing over and over again to you. That's not Him being mean to you, that is Him trying to bless you. If I were you, I would take advantage of the voice of the Lord while you can still hear it and humble yourself to obey Him. Sometimes God does sound like a broken record and most times we still don't hear Him, even when He repeats Himself.

SOMETHING TO SIP ON:

For God speaketh once, yea twice, yet man perceiveth it not.
Job 33:14

Trust not in oppression, and become not vain in robbery: if riches increase, set not your heart upon them.
God hath spoken once; twice have I heard this;
that power belongeth unto God.
Psalms 62:10-11

And Jacob awaked out of his sleep, and he said, Surely the
LORD is in this place; and I knew it not.
Gen 28:16

Then came there a voice from heaven, saying, I have both
glorified it, and will glorify it again.
The people therefore, that stood by, and heard it, said that it
thundered: others said, An angel spake to him.
John 12:28-29

Just because God is speaking, does not mean that everybody
knows it.

Just because you know God is speaking, does not mean that you
automatically understand what God is saying.

It is the glory of God to conceal a thing: but the honour of
kings is to search out a matter.
Prov 25:2

A COIN IN THE TRASH

Every four months or so, we have the incredible privilege of doing a food outreach in the trash dumps of Matamoras, Mexico. Sometime back, our missions team climbed a heap and handed out thousands of pounds of food and put brand new shoes on the feet of kids that may have never seen anything new in their lives. It was awesome.

We preached the Word to a small crowd gathered to wait on the next trash truck. In the midst of that group was a lady named "Anna". Later I would find out that Anna had been dumped there at the age of six by her mother in exchange for a certain dollar amount. Since that day, she had not known anything but stench, filth, and hopelessness for 30 years.

Anna gave her heart to Jesus one Friday. For the first time since she was thrown away as a little girl, she felt the love, joy and peace that only comes from being found by Jesus Christ.

See, in the midst of that horrible place there was something of great value, something priceless. The thing that made Anna move from the dead category to the life category, was that Jesus did not see her as trash. He saw her as precious. All anybody else could see was 30 years of filth, but Jesus saw a heartbroken woman that had been abandoned by her mother and abused by the world. Jesus saw great potential and a precious soul under that dirt. On that Friday, He began to call her out of that mess and clean her up in every way a person can be cleaned.

While I was thinking about this miracle, my good friend, Andy Daly, looked on the ground and found the first of several coins there in the dump. "Look, Pastor" He said, "I found a coin in the trash." That was not the only precious coin found in the dump that Friday. Please remember to pray for Anna when you seek the Lord this week and don't forget to thank God that He sees us as valuable. Even when we live in a dump, He sees the value past the trash.

SOMETHING TO SIP ON:

Jesus sees the value in all of us. Jesus see us as the finished product no matter what stage of life we are in. (Romans 4:17, Judges 6:12)

Hidden riches…..
There are lots of incredible "hidden riches" that most will never find. Being led by the Lord ensures us that we drill our wells in the perfect places for His righteous pay off. (see Jeremiah 33:3)

> *And I will give thee the treasures of darkness, and hidden riches of secret places, that thou mayest know that I, the LORD, which call thee by thy name, am the God of Israel.*
> ### *Isa 45:3*

While you are praying today, you might remember our sister, Anna and the families that live throughout the dumps of the world.

WOODEN WONDER

*And this gospel of the kingdom will be preached in **ALL THE WORLD** as a witness to all the nations, and then the end will come.*
Matt 24:14

According to the order of God, our Master loves to stamp the number FOUR on things having to do with His creation. Four is the number for "*ALL THE WORLD*".

For example:

4 DIRECTIONS:
NORTH SOUTH EAST AND WEST

4 ELEMENTS IN THE WORLD:
EARTH AIR FIRE & WATER

4 OCEANS THAT COVER THE WORLD:
ATLANTIC, PACIFIC, ARCTIC & INDIAN

4 SEASONS IN A YEAR:
SPRING SUMMER FALL WINTER

4 WORLDLY EMPIRES:
BABYLON, MEDO-PERSIAN, GREECE & ROME

4 KINGDOMS:
MINERAL, VEGETABLE, ANIMAL & SPIRITUAL

4 PARTS OF THE ANIMAL KINGDOM:
MAN BEAST, FOWL & FISH

4 LUNAR CYCLES FOR ALL THE WORLD

If you can consider that, consider the fours that are attached to Jesus and the Cross that is for ALL THE WORLD.

There are four crosses (used for hanging) in the world.

The Latin cross: (what we probably think of when you picture a cross and it's the one most likely used as the cross of Christ, with an inscription above His head)

Saint Anthony's cross: (looks like a capital T)

Saint Andrews cross: (looks like a capital X)

Greek Cross: with a center crossbeam (looks like a plus sign)

Jesus was born 4000 years after Adam. Because a day to the Lord is as 1000 years (*2 Peter 3:8*) That makes Him born on the 4th day. Why? Because He was born for ALL THE WORLD.

There are four Gospels that tell the story of Jesus Christ. Because Jesus Christ is born, crucified and resurrected for ALL THE WORLD.

The terms Golgotha and Calvary (the names of the place where Jesus was crucified) are found exactly 4 times in scripture.

Why? Because the geographical location might have been in Israel, but He was crucified for ALL THE WORLD.

There were four soldiers at the cross (John 19:23) They parted His garment into four pieces. (John 19:23)

There are four different interpretations of what was written on the inscription above His head.

THIS IS JESUS THE KING OF THE JEWS.
Matt 27:37

THE KING OF THE JEWS.
Mark 15:26

THIS IS THE KING OF JEWS
LUKE 23:38

JESUS OF NAZZERETH KING OF THE JEWS
JOHN 19:19

A mess up? Not Hardly. This was put there by meticulous design so that ALL THE WORLD would know who this was that was paying the price.

In the Greek, there are exactly 28 (7 x 4) of these words. I think that's neat because the word CROSS appears exactly 28 (7x 4) times in the Bible, as does the word LAMB.

The number 28 represents "times & seasons". That's why in Ecclesiastes there are exactly 28 times and seasons listed there.

Now why would the Holy Spirit have the 40 - 44 different authors of the Bible only write the word cross in the bible 28 times? Out of 810,697 words, only 28 of those words are *cross*. Why?

Because the cross of Jesus guarantees us victory for every time and season we go through. There is a cross for every season of your life. Because the cross is indeed for All THE WORLD, even though only a fragment of the population is for the Savior that hung on it.

If the plan of God is to display the fact that Jesus Christ died for you, and if it is for everybody or ALL THE WORLD, then it makes since to me that God would choose a piece of wood that has four points. Do you realize that when the Roman soldiers laid that cross down on the ground and were nailing Jesus Christ to it, from God's perspective, the cross was pointing to the north, south, east and west? Or I suppose we say, ALL THE WORLD. Why would God do that? Well, you've read it in John 3:16.

SOMETHING TO SIP ON:

There is no power in numbers, for all power and authority has been given unto Jesus. (Matthew 28:18) With that said, numbers are a valuable part of God's lingo in His written Word.

Some excellent books on the subject:

Number in Scripture By E.W. Bullinger
Biblical Mathematics By Ed F. Vallowe
The King James Code & By Divine Order By Michael Hoggard
God The Master Mathematician By Dr. N.W. Hutchings
Numbers That Preach By Troy A. Brewer (that's me)

HARVEST MOON

September 28th's full moon of this last year was a special one. It's known as "The Harvest Moon". I think that's really neat. I'll tell you why in just a minute. But first, let's just take a fun look at the Moon itself.

Many of you know that I am a very amateur star gazer and that I am into the night sky. I can remember getting "the big head" when I aced the 9th grade geography test and identified all 50 states. Just like that, I get a big kick out of pointing up to the night sky and naming the constellations and the stars.

My wife and kids don't like it near as much as I do. Sometimes at night, as we are walking from the driveway to the front door, I will notice the sky is clear and my astronomy juices start flowing. It is well understood in my family that when I begin to say things like "See that bright red star up there, guys?" this is their queue to act like they do not hear me and hurry into the house. Many of those times I will hear the front door shut and then notice I have been talking to myself. They do this to avoid hearing how far away that star is or how that constellation is mentioned in the Bible. I don't blame them.

You might want to run off as well, but before you do, let me make a point. The Moon is a really neat place. Here are some interesting facts about that "Big Pizza Pie" that Dean-O used to sing about.

Cool stuff to know about the Moon:

It's about 280,000 miles away and moves a little bit farther out every year.

The Moon has a 29.5 day orbit and causes the tides of the world to pull towards it because the Moon's gravity pulls on our oceans. High tide aligns with the Moon as the Earth spins underneath. Another high tide occurs on the opposite side of the planet because gravity pulls Earth toward the Moon more than it pulls the water. How cool is that?

Our Moon is bigger than the planet Pluto & roughly one-fourth the diameter of Earth (though I am almost certain that Texas is bigger).

The Moon will have "moon-quakes" from time to time. Small moonquakes that start several miles below the surface happen because of the gravitational pull of Earth.

The Moon's heavily cratered surface is the result of being beat up by space rocks over a long period of time. These craters have not eroded much because there is no wind or rain to erode them. Are you still awake or did you just run into my house with the kids?

One of the neatest things about the Moon is that God designed her so that she always shows us the same face. This is an amazing feature when you consider that the Earth and the Moon are rotating and orbiting. I looked all this up at space.com to see how that can be. They say that long ago, the Earth's gravitational effects slowed the Moon's rotation about its axis. Once the Moon's rotation slowed enough to match its orbital period (the time it takes the Moon to go around Earth) the effect stabilized. I read that and said "hmmmmm" to myself. But of course I didn't really have any idea what in the wild world of sports I just got through reading. Maybe you did.

I like the Moon and I am glad she is there. I will tell you one more really neat thing about the Moon. She is full of light, yet she has no light of her own.

Has anyone ever seen the light of the Moon? No we haven't. We have seen the light of the Sun reflected off of the Moon. How beautiful that light is!

I wish we (the church) were more like the Moon. I believe that we are supposed to be. Our witness will only be as affective as the degree to which we reflect the light of Jesus.

An article in Newsweek titled "The Fall of the Dinosaurs" explored the downfall of corporate giants such as General Motors, IBM, and Sears. Tucked away in the opening remarks were these words: "The institutions of family, church and government have long since lost their luster." Whether the diminished luster is perceived or real, an illustration from Russian scientists may contain the answer. On February 4, 1993, officials at the Flight Control Center near Moscow reported the successful deployment of a space reflector. This aluminum-covered disc was used by cosmonauts in the space station Mir to reflect light from the Sun to the dark side of Earth. With a twenty-five-foot disc in space, they were able to produce a two-mile circle of light on Earth. Such a move placed Russia in the forefront of this reflective technology. If the church has lost its luster, it may be due to our feeble attempts to produce light rather than reflect the Light. How much greater would our impact be if we started being better mirrors of the Son!

That's what we are supposed to be about, reflecting the Light. We, as the body of Christ, do not have anything to offer except for Jesus Christ. Whatever else we are offering, peddling or submitting is not light at all.

Psalms chapter 72:7 promises the abundance of peace "so long as the moon endureth" and I think there is hope for peace in this old world as long as we are willing to reflect His light to others.

According to Rick Warren, there are two basic reasons people don't know Jesus Christ as their Lord and Savior:
   (1) They have never met a Christian.
   (2) They have met a Christian.

Christian influence (reflecting the light) is no small matter.

SOMETHING TO SIP ON:

Ye are the light of the world. A city that is set on an hill cannot be hid.

Neither do men light a candle, and put it under a bushel, but on a candlestick; and it giveth light unto all that are in the house.

Let your light so shine before men, that they may see your good works, and glorify your Father which is in heaven.
Matthew 5:14-16

And art confident that thou thyself art a guide of the blind, a light of them which are in darknes,
Romans 2:19

For ye were sometimes darkness, but now are ye light in the Lord: walk as children of light:
Ephesians 5:8

Do all things without murmurings and disputings: That ye may be blameless and harmless, the sons of God, without rebuke, in the midst of a crooked and perverse nation, among whom ye shine as lights in the world;
Philippians 2:14-15

PASTOR TROY'S TOP 5 WAYS TO GUARANTEE THAT YOUR KIDS WILL USE DRUGS, BE MISERABLE AND BECOME MINDLESS HORMONES

It seems to me that a lot of today's parents are training their kids for a lifetime of failure and they are getting really good at it. After careful observation, I decided to jot down some of these fail proof, guaranteed strategies for raising up a good reason the rest of us lock our doors at night. Here are the top 5.

1. **Do not be faithful and committed in serving God**.

If it is your goal that your kids turn out really bad, it is very important that you stay in bed during service times. Your weekly illustration of the fact that you can only serve God when you are not tired and when it is convenient will go a long way. Convince them that it is not necessary to be committed in service to the Lord and I guarantee you that they will find it hard to be committed and faithful to anything other than what they feel. If you do this already, the devil himself thanks you for your support.

2. **Let your kids hear you complain about those in authority**.

Every time you pass a policeman you should say something derogatory. Be sure and voice your hateful opinions about the government. If your child is having problems at school, it is very important that you disrespect that teacher in front of your kid. If your little boy's team looses, you have got to "trash" the coach in a way that makes a memory and it won't take much. Your words and the way you treat authority will sear their little attitude for a lifetime. Oh and by all means, you must not forget to tell your kids how churches have done you wrong and how you disagree with every little thing you didn't order from the pulpit. If you do this, the devil himself thanks you for your support in teaching your kids to be unteachable.

3. Have rules with out relationship.

Be somebody that lays down the law, but never gives a hug or an encouraging word. As soon as you come into the house, point out what rules have been broken and then after you throw your fit, disappear to some other place where you pretend you do not have any kids. Do not have a clue what your child's interests are or what is going on in his or her life. Just constantly chant your list of demands and how they never meet your standards. If you can do this for even a short time during those vulnerable years, I can guarantee your teenager will seek out relationships through sexual activity, and peace of mind through a pipe or a bottle. The devil himself knows that rules without relationship leads to rebellion and he thanks you for your support.

4. Have relationship without rules.

Dads, don't look at your boy as your son but treat him as your "running buddy". Let him sip your beer and take him to "R" rated movies when he is ten. Let him watch anything he wants to on video tape. Let him hear you talk bad about his mama. Slap him on the back when you hear he has been in a fight and tell him that getting in the backseat of a car with another little girl is all a part of growing up.

Moms, be sure and look at your daughter like she is your "girlfriend". Discuss things with her that you should only say to adults. Tell her how sorry the men in your life have been. Encourage her to dress in a provocative way. Take her down to the doctor, put her on birth control pills and then look her in the eye and explain to her that this is "being responsible".

If you can do these things, sooner or later they won't think you're cool anymore. Relationship without rules leads to rebellion. If you want to absolutely guarantee your kid's misery in the future, give them no rules, no boundaries and encourage them in "expressing their feelings". This is very important to the devil's plan for your child's life and if you are actively participating, he thanks you for your support.

5. **Never grow up.**

This last one is easy. Keep yourself in a time warp and act the same way, listen to the same music, do the same things you did before you had kids. Do not progress, do not advance, just remain eighteen forever. If you want your kids to be unbalanced, ill responsible adults, all you have to do is set that example now by refusing to change. Don't put your kids well being ahead of yours, be who you have always been and celebrate it! Keep toking on your joint and banging your head! All you have to do to curse your kids into failure is be the same way today as you were twenty years ago. If that's you, the devil himself thanks you for your support.

For those of you that are struggling to raise miserable, drug addicts and mindless hormones, I hope this list has served to help you. I also hope and sincerely pray that you will loose your influence over your kids before the rest of us are cleaning up your terrible mess.

If you are trying to raise your kids to be happy, young adults that love life and the God that gives it, I hope that you will judge yourself as a parent against this list. If you find yourself guilty of even one of these things, it is not too late. Cry out to the Lord, pray for your kids and for the wisdom to raise them. Change your life and give your kids a fighting chance. Your selfless love for your children will make an eternal difference that will outlast the curse of the parents that couldn't.

SOMETHING TO SIP ON:

And the LORD said, "Shall I hide from Abraham what I am doing, since Abraham shall surely become a great and mighty nation, and all the nations of the earth shall be blessed in him? For I have known him, in order that he may command his children and his household after him, that they keep the way of the LORD, to do righteousness and justice, that the LORD may bring to Abraham what He has spoken to him."
Gen 18:17-20 NKJV

And these words, which I command thee this day, shall be in thine heart: And thou shalt teach them diligently unto thy children, and shalt talk of them when thou sittest in thine house, and when thou walkest by the way, and when thou liest down, and when thou risest up.
Deuteronomy 6:6-7 KJV

And he took a child, and set him in the midst of them: and when
he had taken him in his arms, he said unto them,
Whosoever shall receive one of such children in my name,
receiveth me: and whosoever shall receive me,
receiveth not me, but him that sent me.
Mark 9:36-37 KJV

And Jesus called a little child unto him,
and set him in the midst of them,
And said, Verily I say unto you, Except ye be converted,
and become as little children,
ye shall not enter into the kingdom of heaven.
Whosoever therefore shall humble himself as this little child,
the same is greatest in the kingdom of heaven.
And whoso shall receive one such little child
in my name receiveth me.
But whoso shall offend one of these little ones which believe in
me, it were better for him that a millstone were hanged about
his neck, and that he were drowned in the depth of the sea.
Matt 18:2-6 KJV

ABSORBING THE ASTOUNDING

I read this quote in TIME today and thought I would share it with you.

"An elderly woman I know was at lunch at a great resort one day before World War I began. Suddenly from the sky, one of those new flying machines, an aeroplane, which no one there had ever seen, zoomed in to land on the smooth, rolling lawn. Everyone ran out to look at this marvel and touch it. What, she was asked 70 years later, did you do after that? "We went inside and finished lunch."

The Berlin wall is down. "Ho-hum". We have spacecraft on Mars. "Yeah, I know." Everybody carries phones with them now. "Um-hm." I am in Texas today and will be in Africa tomorrow. "Yeah, that's cool", you say as you reach for the remote.

We have an amazing ability to just absorb and somewhat dismiss the absolutely astounding. I think part of it is a defense mechanism against all the extreme hell we go through in our lives, but I think that the majority of it is our flesh and not the friend of GOD. How de-synthesized are you to the following statement?

"HE IS RISEN"

I encourage you to invade that part of your brain that is reserved for the last episode of ALIAS or THE SHEILD with this truth and let it really mean something to you. Set a time aside to let the Holy Ghost show you what a big deal it is that Jesus Christ slapped death in the face once and for all time. Meditate on it. Mentally chew on it. Take it to the bank and celebrate it.

How about this one:

YOU ARE SAVED & BORN AGAIN

Excuse me, do you know what a big deal that is? Do you know how easy it is to dismiss such an incredible statement? Do we realize that a lot better people than us never had the truth revealed to them? God help us to make a big deal out of those things that are in fact a very big deal. God help us not to just absorb what otherwise should be absolutely astounding and let us truly be thankful.

SOMETHING TO SIP ON:

The Word says that when we dismiss the awesome things God has done for us, our imaginations tend to go south. The directions we go when we do, will always land us into foolishness and hurt.

Because that, when they knew God, they glorified him not as God, neither were thankful; but became vain in their imaginations, and their foolish heart was darkened. Professing themselves to be wise, they became fools.
Rom 1:21-22

WHEN THE BLESSING IS A CURSE

I have thought about it in Central America and in east Africa. I have cried about it in the trash dumps of Matamoras, Mexico. It is a subject that keeps coming up in my life.

I spent several hours flying over the Sahara Desert a few weeks ago and I looked down at a few tiny villages scattered across what looked more like the surface of Mars than the Earth and I started to think about it again.

"Why are some of us so blessed, when so many are not?"

"Why am I so fat, when so many others are starving?"

"Why am I in a comfortable quad engined jet 39,000 feet above somebody in a filthy desert tent? Somebody better than me. Most likely smarter than me. Why am I so blessed, when so many are not?"

At that very moment my mind focused on the great day of reckoning and on the day where Jesus sets the record straight. A terrible epiphany hit my grey matter and I realized for the first time that a lot of people are going to curse their blessing on that day.

One after another will curse the day they were born in America because it enabled them to live a life without being desperate for Jesus. Some people will curse the fact that they had money in the bank, because it enabled them to not have to cry out to the

Lord for His provision. Others will curse their healthy bodies and even their loving families because those simple comforts put them in a place where they never felt the need to truly seek after the presence of the God we all so desperately need.

On the other hand and on that same day, millions will be stretching their hands toward the throne and thanking God for the unfair deal they got in this short lifetime. They will bless the curse that made them realize that they were pitiful people in desperate need of a Savior.

The key to this life and the one beyond, is learning how to be blessed while remaining totally dependant on Jesus. This way our blessings are a blessing and not something that curses us.

SOMETHING TO SIP ON:

When king David got time off from terrible war and leisured on his balcony, his eyes fell on Bathsheba and that blessing became a curse that cost him 4 of his children and years of strife.

When Samson was anointed to be stronger and faster than any other human being, he began to get arrogant and think he didn't need to stay holy before God. What should have been a blessing became a curse that cost him his anointing, his eyesight and twenty years of judging Israel.

Blessings are only blessings as long as we don't use them as an excuse to get out from under the presence of God.

And when he was gone forth into the way, there came one running, and kneeled to him, and asked him, Good Master, what shall I do that I may inherit eternal life? And Jesus said unto him, Why callest thou me good? there is

none good but one, that is, God.
Thou knowest the commandments, Do not commit adultery, Do
not kill, Do not steal, Do not bear false witness, Defraud not,
Honour thy father and mother.
And he answered and said unto him, Master,
all these have I observed from my youth.
Then Jesus beholding him loved him, and said unto him, One
thing thou lackest: go thy way, sell whatsoever thou hast, and
give to the poor, and thou shalt have treasure in heaven: and
come, take up the cross, and follow me.
And he was sad at that saying, and went away grieved:
for he had great possessions.
And Jesus looked round about, and saith unto his disciples,
How hardly shall they that have riches
enter into the kingdom of God!
Mark 10:17-23 KJV

SPARKS WILL FLY

On the early morning hours of November 1st, my youth facility burned to the ground. We had just had our "To Hell with Halloween" concert when the Evil empire struck back a few hours later. The good news is that the insurance was sound and we are about to begin the rebuilding process. I asked the guys to change the scripture on the marquee to Job 5:7…

Yet man is born unto trouble, as the sparks fly upward.
As sure as heat rises, you can count on trouble in this world. There has to be a place in all of us where we eventually understand that this is not a good world where bad things happen, but rather a broken and messed up world where good things can happen.

There is a day coming where Jesus will flip the script on how things operate in this world, but until then, you can count on trouble. Don't be scared of your day of trouble. Ephesians 6 says that we need to armor up right now, so that when that day slaps us in the face, we can stand and not fall.

God has not called you to hang in there, you are vulnerable when you are hanging from something. God has called you to STAND.

It is a fact that you can count on trouble, but it is the TRUTH that you can count on Jesus, trouble or not.

I choose to live by the truth and not just by the facts. The Truth always will supersede the facts, because Jesus is the way, the TRUTH and the life.

SOMETHING TO SIP ON:

These things I have spoken unto you, that in me ye might have peace. In the world ye shall have tribulation: but be of good cheer; I have overcome the world.
John 16:33

If ye were of the world, the world would love his own: but because ye are not of the world, but I have chosen you out of the world, therefore the world hateth you.
Remember the word that I said unto you,
The servant is not greater than his lord.
If they have persecuted me, they will also persecute you; if they have kept my saying, they will keep yours also.
But all these things will they do unto you for my name's sake, because they know not him that sent me.
If I had not come and spoken unto them, they had not had sin: but now they have no cloke for their sin.
He that hateth me hateth my Father also.
John 15:19-23 KJV

Confirming the souls of the disciples, and exhorting them to continue in the faith, and that we must through much tribulation enter into the kingdom of God.
Acts 14:22 KJV

*Yea, and all that will live godly in Christ Jesus
shall suffer persecution.*
2 Tim 3:12 KJV

*By faith Moses, when he was come to years, refused to be
called the son of Pharaoh's daughter; Choosing rather to suffer
affliction with the people of God, than to enjoy the pleasures of
sin for a season;*
Heb 11:24-25 KJV

*Be sober, be vigilant; because your adversary the devil, as a
roaring lion, walketh about, seeking whom he may devour:
Whom resist stedfast in the faith, knowing that the same
afflictions are accomplished in your brethren that are in the
world. But the God of all grace, who hath called us unto his
eternal glory by Christ Jesus, after that ye have suffered a
while, make you perfect, stablish, strengthen, settle you.
To him be glory and dominion for ever and ever. Amen.*
1 Peter 5:8-11 KJV

DISASTER RELIEF

I saw a neat article on the Associated Press that had a lot to say about how people suggest the government should stop the onslaught of hurricanes coming into our country. In our generation's way of thinking, the government is kind of like Mom and Dad, so of course they should protect us from ugly hurricanes. See, amateur hurricane-busters have come up with any number of crackpot ideas to spare our coasts from storms. Among them are things like blowing hurricanes away with giant fans or blowing them up with nuclear warheads. I think the latter is a suggestion born more out of frustration than anything else.

Even the federal government has thrown its hat into the ring with three decades of ill-fated research called *"Project Stormfury"*. This of course, before shelving the idea of weather modification altogether in the 1980s. (Or so they say, I whisper under my breath.)

But dozens of ideas continue to crop up among weather bugs, internet junkies and other people that think they have come up with a way to spare coastal residents the terrible misery of hurricanes.

Some of these suggestions have included coating the surface of the water with olive oil, towing an iceberg down to Florida to cool down the water temperature, or building large fans on the coast to blow away approaching storms. By far, the most outlandish proposal to raise an eyebrow, and one that continues to pop back up every year, is the idea to use a nuclear warhead to blow a hurricane out of the water.

"Hurricanes are bad enough without being radioactive," one official said. "Put that genie back in the bottle. Nuclear weapons are more dangerous than hurricanes."

What's real is that all of us would love to divert the storms that chase us down. There is a part of all of us that wants to unleash nuclear vengeance on the storms that threaten us. I know I do. As Americans deal with three major hurricanes in less than 30 days, it strikes me as a spiritual parallel to the day that we live in and what a dangerous day it is.

Not just on a national level, but on a very personal level, the things that come against us are bigger and meaner and come more frequent, than those charted out by the generations before us. The potential for horrific disaster is greater today than ever before. The storms that tear into us don't come with names like Charlie, Frances and Ivan, they blow up into our lives as bankruptcy, disease and marital problems.

One day you can look up through clear blue skies and then the next day get hit with the tempest of unemployment or even the report of cancer. You never saw it coming, you didn't hear it in the forecast, but nonetheless the storm is there and it changes everything.

I've got good news and bad news that I wish everybody would hear. The *bad news* is that storms will come. As sure as sparks fly upwards, the Bible says, you're going to have trouble. Just like the crackpots I mentioned at the beginning of this, a lot of people have crazy ideas as how to fend off the squalls that approach us. There is no need for you to try and invent some way to ward off the mess that is after you. Jesus Christ has provided the answer and in no less of an answer than His very self.

The *good news* is, that when Jesus was in the middle of a storm, He was seen walking on the very waves that threatened everybody else. If I am going to face storms, and I am, then I want to be closer to Jesus than ever before.

What is the storm, compared to the God that walks on it?

The Bible relays a story of the disciples finding themselves in a terrible mess while on the Sea of Galilee. From out of nowhere the sky turned black and the waves got huge, so much in fact, that after a little while they were convinced they would never make it to shore. One by one, panic began to take hold and terror took over. The storm was furious, things were terrible and everybody on board was convinced that this was the one that would send them down for good. Everybody that is, but Jesus. Not only was Jesus not panicking, He was not even bothered. He was having a nap!

And, behold, there arose a great tempest in the sea, insomuch
that the ship was covered with the waves: but he was asleep.
And his disciples came to him, and awoke him, saying, Lord,
save us: we perish. And he saith unto them, Why are ye fearful,
O ye of little faith? Then he arose,
and rebuked the winds and the sea;
and there was a great calm. But the men marvelled,
saying, What manner of man is this, that even the winds
and the sea obey him!
Matt 8:24-27

Jesus asked the disciples "Why are you fearful?" The disciples asked another, "What kind of a man is this that has control over the storms and the sea?"

Both of these are very good questions and they both tie in together.

Why are you afraid of the storm if the God that rules the storm is in the same boat that you are in? How can the boat sink if Jesus is in it? So maybe we should ask one more question as we see the next set of hurricanes approaching the radar of our lives.

Are we in the same boat that Jesus is in? If not, we had better be.

SOMETHING TO SIP ON:

And fear not them which kill the body,
but are not able to kill the soul:
but rather fear him which is able to
destroy both soul and body in hell.
Matt 10:28 KJV

COMFORT & CONVICTION

Several years ago a preacher moved to Houston, Texas. Some weeks after he arrived, he had occasion to ride the bus from his home to the downtown area. When he sat down, he discovered that the driver had accidentally given him a quarter too much change.

As he considered what to do, he thought to himself, you better give the quarter back. It would be wrong to keep it. Then he thought, "Oh, forget it, it's only a quarter. Who would worry about this little amount? Anyway, the bus company already gets too much fare; they will never miss it. Accept it as a gift from God and keep quiet."

When his stop came, he paused momentarily at the door, then he handed the quarter to the driver and said, "Here, you gave me too much change."

The driver with a smile, replied, "Aren't you the new preacher in town? I have been thinking lately about going to worship somewhere. I just wanted to see what you would do if I gave you too much change."

When the preacher stepped off the bus, he literally grabbed the nearest light pole, and held on, and said, "O God, I almost sold your Son for a quarter."

SOMETHING TO SIP ON:

In John 16: 7 & 8 Jesus calls the Holy Spirit the comforter and then in the next verse He calls Him the reprover or the convictor. You see it again and again when Jesus addresses the seven Asian churches, a solid balance of conviction and then comfort.

The 1st verse of Isaiah 58 is all about conviction and then the 2nd verse is all about comfort. We need to never be afraid to let the Holy Spirit convict us before He comforts us.

COMFORT WITHOUT CONVICTION IS A DANGEROUS THING

My son, despise not the chastening of the LORD;
neither be weary of his correction:
For whom the LORD loveth he correcteth;
even as a father the son in whom he delighteth.
Happy is the man that findeth wisdom,
and the man that getteth understanding.
Prov 3:11-13 KJV

And ye have forgotten the exhortation which speaketh unto you
as unto children, My son, despise not thou the chastening of the
Lord, nor faint when thou art rebuked of him:
For whom the Lord loveth he chasteneth,
and scourgeth every son whom he receiveth.
If ye endure chastening, God dealeth with you as with sons;
for what son is he whom the father chasteneth not?
But if ye be without chastisement, whereof all are partakers,
then are ye bastards, and not sons.
Furthermore we have had fathers of our flesh which corrected
us, and we gave them reverence: shall we not much rather be in
subjection unto the Father of spirits, and live?

For they verily for a few days chastened us after their own pleasure;
but he for our profit, that we might be partakers of his holiness.
Now no chastening for the present seemeth to be joyous, but
grievous: nevertheless afterward it yieldeth the peaceable fruit
of righteousness unto them which are exercised thereby.
Wherefore lift up the hands which hang down,
and the feeble knees;
And make straight paths for your feet,
lest that which is lame be turned out of the way;
but let it rather be healed.
Heb 12:5-13 KJV

The Brewer's Prayer

"Lord, please put up with me when I reach out for your comfort and kick at your conviction. Please patiently deal with me in those sad times when I am so brainless that I actually think for a moment that I can dictate to you who you are supposed to be and refuse to let you tell me who I am supposed to be. Convict me, comfort me, correct and hug me just don't give up on me. I love you, Lord."

WHO YA GONNA CALL?

In 1982 you could find me on the 9th grade campus of big time Joshua High School. I was the obnoxious kid in cowboy boots and the biggest afro of any one person in Johnson County. My mom would drop me off a couple of hours before school started as she was on her way to nursing school. I would sit out there in the predawn light waiting for the sun to come up and listening to my "boom box". Consequently, I became a kind of 80's music buff.

The 1980's produced a number of one-hit wonders, including the infamous Tommy Tutone and its 1982 hit song "Jenny (867-5309)." This San Francisco band doesn't appear to have made much of a mark on the music world, and it likely wouldn't now be remembered at all were it not for the furor raised by its use of a phone number in its one memorable song.

In "Jenny," a young man laments not having the courage to dial a number found scribbled on a wall and in the chorus they say that number over and over again. Though not explicitly stated in the lyrics, it's strongly implied that the name and number were harvested from a bathroom wall. This would imply "Jenny" is a gal of easy virtue and is to be had for the price of a phone call.

Millions of people have heard that song since 1982 and all of that is fine, unless of course, your number is 867-5309. While that one song might have made Tommy Tutone some money, it has caused nothing but grief for telephone customers unlucky enough to have that combination of numbers as their own. Its relentless chorus pounded the phone number into the minds of teenagers everywhere, resulting in waves of kids dialing it and asking for Jenny. The joke quickly became old for those who had the number and weren't interested in talking to nasty minded teenagers and otherwise mindless hormones.

Even as recently as 1999, phone customers cursed to have been assigned an 867-5309 number were still getting plenty of crank calls. An article from Brown University's newspaper explained what happened when the school added an 867 exchange in the fall of 1999:

The biggest complaints about the new phone exchange, it stated, come from Nina Clemente and Jahanaz Mirza, the two students with "Jenny's" number.

"It's so annoying," Nina said. "It's the worst number to have in the world." The girls receive an average of five "stupid" messages every day on their machine, in addition to a slew of hang-ups.

"It's as if they are really expecting Jenny to pick up the phone," Clemente said.

Just like that, last year when Jim Carrey starred in his movie, "Bruce Almighty", the writers of the script gave God a phone number that Carrey could dial to talk with the Almighty. But instead of using the 555 prefix that movie makers and TV shows generally give phone numbers – they gave God a 776 prefix. A lot of people who saw the movie wrote the number down and started dialing it. One lady in St. Petersburg, Florida received 20 calls an hour from people who wanted to talk to God.

What is God's phone number? I would think that a better prefix for dialing up God would be a 333 instead of a 776. In Jeremiah 33:3 God declares:

> *Call to me and I will answer you and tell you great and unsearchable things you do not know.*
> **Jeremiah 33:3**

God does have a hotline, but a big part of dialing Him has to do with our ability to humble ourselves and admit that He's God. That might sound silly to you, but it's something that most Americans can't seem to do. The problem with calling out to God and admitting that He IS God means that we have to admit that we are NOT God. Most people will never pick up the phone because of that very issue.

God wants us to call on Him and as He says in Jeremiah 33:3 He is willing to answer. I don't know about you, but I tend to wear my caller I.D. out and there are a lot of calls I don't want to answer. (especially at the end of the month when my bills are due.) God is not like us. He doesn't care who we are. If we will humble ourselves and call on Him, He will answer.

I believe that Jesus is looking 24/7 for people that will humble themselves and admit that they are desperate for Him in their lives. This belief prompts me to want to exclaim, "Put your face on the floor and pick up the phone!"

There is a famous verse in the Old Testament that talks about the importance of calling upon the Lord even upon a national basis. This is what it says:

If my people, which are called by my name, shall humble themselves, and pray, and seek my face, and turn from their wicked ways; then will I hear from heaven, and will forgive their sin, and will heal their land.
2 Chronicles 7:14

In the USA, when we need emergency help, we call upon the authorities by dialing 911. It's a number you dial when in the most desperate of circumstances. You don't just sit in your house and let it burn, you call 911. You don't just hide under the covers and let them break into your house, you dial 911. You don't just let that person die of a heart attack, you dial 911. When you need help from the authority that is able to help, we dial 911. To Americans, 911 means an urgent call for help to a place where we can expect a quick and proper response.

I believe that God, being our protective authority, is standing by, waiting for us as a nation to call upon Him. He is willing to protect us and heal us, but we have to be willing to call upon Him for help.

You do remember what happened on 9-11, don't you? Or have you already forgotten?

SOMETHING TO SIP ON:

But from there you will seek the LORD your God, and you will find Him if you seek Him with all your heart and with all your soul.
Deuteronomy 4:29-30 NKJV

Call upon Me in the day of trouble;
I will deliver you, and you shall glorify Me.
Psalms 50:15 NKJV

Because he has set his love upon Me, therefore I will deliver him; I will set him on high, because he has known My name. He shall call upon Me, and I will answer him; I will be with him in trouble; I will deliver him and honor him. With long life I will satisfy him, And show him My salvation.
Psalms 91:14-16 NKJV

Then you will call upon Me and go and pray to Me, and I will listen to you. And you will seek Me and find Me, when you search for Me with all your heart. I will be found by you, says the LORD, and I will bring you back from your captivity;
Jeremiah 29:12-14 NKJV

CAPTURED BY THE CAUSE

Winston Churchill was one of the great leaders of the World War II era. He understood the law of the "big picture".

It is said that during World War II, when Britain was experiencing its darkest days, the country had a difficult time keeping men working in the coal mines. Many wanted to give up their dirty, thankless jobs in the dangerous mines to join the military service, which garnered much public praise and support. Yet their work in the mines was critical to the success of the war. Without coal, the military and the people at home would be in trouble. So the prime minister faced thousands of coal miners one day and told them of their importance to the war effort, how their role could make or break the goal of maintaining England's freedom.

Churchill painted a picture of what it would be like when the war ended, of the grand parade that would honor the people who fought the war. First would come the sailors of the navy, he said, the people who continued the tradition of Trafalgar and the defeat of the Spanish Armada. Next would come the best and brightest of Britain, the pilots of the Royal Air Force who fended off the German Air Forces. Following them would be the soldiers who had fought at Dunkirk. Then last of all would come the coal-dust-covered men in miners' caps. Churchill then indicated that someone from the crowd might say, "And where were you during the critical days of the struggle?" And the voices of 10 thousand men would respond, "We were deep in the earth with our faces to the coal."

It's said that tears appeared in the eyes of those hardened men and they returned to their inglorious work with steely resolve, having been reminded of the role they were playing in their country's noble goal of preserving freedom for the Western World.

Those men, on that day, knew what it was to be captured by the cause of freedom. They were able to go back to their thankless and difficult jobs because they understood that they were a valuable part of something much, much bigger than themselves.

LET IT SO BE WITH ALL OF US IN THE KINGDOM OF GOD.

SOMETHING TO SIP ON:

A big part of being led by the Spirit of God means being a part of miniscule tasks. Things that do not seem like they are that big of a deal. Places where there is no "amen corner" or fanfare or a salute from your peers.

To be captured by the cause means to be a team player and big picture kind of thinker. Our jobs may be small and unappreciated by most but that does not mean that rewards us any less. Look at what Jesus said and consider how considerate our Savior truly is.

For whosoever shall give you a cup of water to drink in my name, because ye belong to Christ, verily I say unto you, he shall not lose his reward.
Mark 9:41

THE SOMEDAY SYNDROME

Do you not say, 'There are still four months
and then comes the harvest'?...
John 4:35 NKJV

One of the mentalities that Jesus constantly confronted in His day is the same that we deal with in ours. I call it the someday syndrome. It's the thinking that everything God has for us is the distant future. It's when we get too caught up (pardon the pun) looking for the rapture or some future great event and we miss the obvious move of God that is for the RIGHT NOW. Look at these examples of how Jesus dealt with the someday syndrome.

Martha said, (and I paraphrase) "Someday in the far off future, my brother Lazarus will be raised."

JESUS SAID, "I AM THE RESURRECTION AND THE LIFE." John 11:25

The thief on the Cross said (and I paraphrase) "Someday way off in the distant future when you enter into your Kingdom, will you somehow look back and remember me?"

JESUS SAID, "THIS DAY YOU WILL BE WITH ME IN PARADISE." Luke 23:43

The Woman at the well said, (and I paraphrase) "Someday, a long time from now, when the messiah finally shows up, He will reveal all things."

JESUS SAID, (and I paraphrase) "THAT'S ME, AND I AM SPEAKING TO YOU RIGHT NOW." John 4:26

Jesus flat out says, do not say that in four months there will be a harvest. Do not say that someday soon I will make a difference or one of these days God's gonna use me. Quit looking at yourself and look up right now and see that you are standing in the midst of a great harvest.

Someday is here right now!

SOMETHING TO SIP ON:

*Seek ye the LORD while he may be found, call ye upon him
while he is near: Let the wicked forsake his way,
and the unrighteous man his thoughts:
and let him return unto the LORD,
and he will have mercy upon him; and to our God,
for he will abundantly pardon.
For my thoughts are not your thoughts,
neither are your ways my ways, saith the LORD.
For as the heavens are higher than the earth, so are my ways
higher than your ways, and my thoughts than your thoughts.*
Isa 55:6-9 KJV

Now is the accepted time; behold, now is the day of salvation.
2 Cor 6:2

GERONIMO

Don't think for a minute that you have heaven's roster figured out. When we finally get home, there are going to be people there you were sure would not make it. Let me tell you a story about one of those people (other than me).

A long time before there were any caged animals in southern Oklahoma there was a zoo. People paid big bucks to gawk and poke, not at an exotic animal but at a man. A man named Geronimo.

The American Indian warrior had found himself captured and forced to spend the last years of his life as a prisoner and as a trophy of the government that had caught him. He sat day after day in a cold room in the midst of Fort Sill while people lined up to take a look at him. He suffered seeing the ugly looks and the hateful remarks day after day. It must have been like a horrible nightmare for him.

He was a man without a people, a man without a country, a man without a nation and man without any hope. He had been defeated in every way a person can be defeated. His heart was so broken, I don't know if any of us can really understand the depths of despair he must have felt.

One day a Christian visited him. That same somebody had the nerve, the audacity, and the shrewd political incorrectness to share the love of Jesus Christ with that desperate man. For the first time in his life, he began to understand that all was not lost because this was not his home. When the love of Jesus Christ was presented to him, he put his face on the floor and called Jesus Lord.

Geronimo spent the rest of his last days giving his testimony how that the Lord had healed him of bitterness. When people would come to see him, he would say, "I don't want to be known as a warrior I want to be known as a servant."

Heaven is not the place you go to when you leave home. Heaven is the home you go to when you leave this place. You're going to be surprised at who you see when you get home.

*After this I beheld, and, lo, a great multitude, which no man
could number, of all nations, and kindreds, and people,
and tongues, stood before the throne, and before the Lamb,
clothed with white robes, and palms in their hands;
And cried with a loud voice, saying, Salvation to our God
which sitteth upon the throne, and unto the Lamb.
And all the angels stood round about the throne,
and about the elders and the four beasts,
and fell before the throne on their faces, and worshipped God,
Saying, Amen: Blessing, and glory, and wisdom, and
thanksgiving, and honour, and power, and might, be unto our
God for ever and ever. Amen.*
Rev 7:9-12 KJV

AN ACCURATE STANDARD

In Washington D.C. there is a building called the "National Institute of Standards & Technology." This facility is responsible for storing perfect samples of weights and measurements. They have what are called "prototypes" of pound weights and kilograms. Measuring rods for feet, yards & metric measurements like meters. For example, they have a "Meter Standard"; a reinforced bar of platinum alloyed with exactly 10% iridium. When they want to know the exact measurement of a "meter" they cool this bar down to 0 degrees Celsius at a sea level of 45 degrees latitude then they know they will have the exact tip to tip measurement of a meter. That bar is known as "prototype #27", because the original is kept in a suburb of Paris at the International Bureau of Weights & Measures.

We Christians also have a measuring rod that never changes. 2 Timothy 3:16-17 tells us: "All scripture is given by inspiration of God, and is profitable for doctrine, for reproof, for correction, for instruction in righteousness: That the man of God may be perfect, thoroughly furnished unto all good works."

Jesus said in another place that the scriptures do testify of Him. It is Jesus Christ that is the perfect standard for everything in your life that needs measured. I encourage you to grab ahold of Jesus and don't let go!

SOMETHING TO SIP ON:

A look at the accurate standard:

According to statistics from Wycliffe International, the Society of Gideons, and the International Bible Society, the number of new Bibles that are sold, given away, or otherwise distributed in the United States is about 168,000 per day.

The Bible can be read aloud in 70 hours.

There are 8,674 different Hebrew words in the Bible, 5,624 different Greek words, and 12,143 different English words in the King James Version.

A number of verses in the Bible (KJV) contain all but 1 letter of the alphabet: Ezra 7:21 contains all but the letter j; Joshua 7:24, 1 Kings 1:9, 1 Chronicles 12:40, 2 Chronicles 36:10, Ezekiel 28:13, Daniel 4:37, and Haggai 1:1 contain all but q; 2 Kings 16:15 and 1 Chronicles 4:10 contain all but z; and Galatians 1:14 contains all but k.

BIBLE STATISTICS:

Number of books in the Bible: 66
Total Chapters: 1,189
Total Verses: 31,102
Words: 788,258
Number of promises given in the Bible: 1,260

Commands: 6,468
Predictions: over 8,000
Fulfilled prophecy: 3,268 verses
Unfulfilled prophecy: 3,140
Number of questions: 3,294
Longest name: Mahershalalhashbaz (Isaiah 8:1)
Longest verse: Esther 8:9 (78 words)
Shortest verse: John 11:35 (2 words: "Jesus wept").
Middle chapter: Psalm 117
Shortest chapter (by number of words): Psalm 117
Longest book: Psalms (150 chapters)
Shortest book (by number of words): 3 John
Longest chapter: Psalm 119 (176 verses)
Number of times the word "God" appears: 3,358
Number of times the word "Lord" appears: 7,736
Number of different authors: 40 (perhaps 44)
Number of languages the Bible has been translated into: over
1,200

The following 17 verses from the King James Version are
completely gone from the New International Version and other
modern translations.

Howbeit this kind goeth not out but by prayer and fasting.
Matthew 17:21 (KJV)

Take a look in your N.I.V. and see for yourself. They completely
omit it! How can we say that we will rely on the accurate standard
of the Word of God if we are not even willing to keep the standard
itself accurate? God help us to take His Word seriously enough
to translate it in a reliable and accurate way.   Here are sixteen
other verses that you will not find in a New International Version
or in like minded translations. I am not even tapping into the
hundreds, if not thousands, of words left out, it is enough for this
point to list the entire scriptures that they omitted.

Matthew 18:11
For the Son of man is come to save that which was lost.

Matthew 23:14
Woe unto you, scribes and Pharisees, hypocrites! for ye devour widows' houses, and for a pretence make long prayer: therefore ye shall receive the greater damnation.

Mark 7:16
If any man have ears to hear, let him hear.

Mark 9:44 & Mark 9:46
Where their worm dieth not, and the fire is not quenched.

Mark 11:26
But if ye do not forgive, neither will your Father which is in heaven forgive your trespasses.

Mark 15:28
And the scripture was fulfilled, which saith, And he was numbered with the transgressors.

Luke 17:36
Two men shall be in the field; the one shall be taken, and the other left.

Luke 23:17
For of necessity he must release one unto them at the feast.

John 5:4
For an angel went down at a certain season into the pool, and troubled the water: whosoever then first after the troubling of the water stepped in was made whole of whatsoever disease he had.

Acts 8:37
And Philip said, If thou believest with all thine heart, thou mayest. And he answered and said, I believe that Jesus Christ is the Son of God.

Acts 15:34
Notwithstanding it pleased Silas to abide there still.

Acts 24:7
But the chief captain Lysias came upon us, and with great violence took him away out of our hands,

Acts 28:29
And when he had said these words, the Jews departed, and had great reasoning among themselves.

Romans 16:24
The grace of our Lord Jesus Christ be with you all. Amen.

I John 5:7
For there are three that bear record in heaven, the Father, the Word, and the Holy Ghost: and these three are one.

A WINNER EITHER WAY

According to my earnest expectation and my hope,
that in nothing I shall be ashamed,
but that with all boldness, as always,
so now also Christ shall be magnified in my body,
whether it be by life, or by death.
For to me to live is Christ, and to die is gain.
Philippians 1:20-21

I went to see a friend in the hospital tonight. His doctors tell him that he only has days, if not hours, left to live. That's not a fun thing to hear and I wondered how I would find him when I got there. Would he be awake? If he was awake, would he want to talk? If he did want to talk, how would that go? You have to put a clamp on your head and not let your thoughts run down those rabbit trails. I said a prayer under my breath and turned the corner from the elevator, confident that Jesus was with both of us.

Hugely Hospital's ICU was buzzing with the terrible business of trauma and suffering as the nurse pointed me to the right room. There he was, tubes all over with a monitor beeping in the background and a great big smile on his face. I don't think I have ever been so happy to see teeth on a man.

He was genuinely happy to see me and the peace he had at that moment was authentic. A true testimony to how good God is, even in the very worst of times. Leo always has been a happy kind of guy. He painted several murals in our youth facility, as well as some Burleson schools and he did it with a smile on is face. I was hoping he would smile and true to form, he did.

I told him I wasn't ready to bury him yet, but nonetheless we could talk turkey about the things that go through a dying man's heart. For the next 20 minutes we discussed spiritually intimate things and took care of some "business".

When I left there, I drove west down Hwy 1187 into a beautiful sunset and I wondered how many other people besides Leo were visiting the sunset of their own lives. So I sat here at this computer to look it up. Let's take a look at it.

WORLD MORTALITY RATE

1.78	per second
107	per minute
6390	per hour
153 thousand	per day
56.0 million	per year
3.9 billion	per average lifetime (70 years)

Source biblehelp.com

Every day there are 153 thousand funerals throughout the world. If you live to be 70 years old you will see 3.9 billion people around you take their last breath. If you have any friends at all, you will stand at the grave of a lost loved one sooner or later. All of them painful, all of them tragic, but there is a division between them. Though we all experience sundown, and while we all encounter grief, there are those who have hope in Christ and those who do not. There are those who have the promise of resurrection life and those who do not. There are those who have eternal life in Jesus and those who do not. It's really a simple distinction. There are those who have death in death and those who have life in death.

As my good friend Steve Jones put it, "Jesus not only died for our sins, but He slapped death in the face." The hand that slapped death had a nail scar in it and this is what we remember as we face our sunsets in life.

This same year another friend, Gina Moore met Jesus face to face on a day that none of us anticipated. Unlike Brother Leo, we had no idea that Gina was facing her sundown. But Gina faced her first glimpse of heaven the same way she faced every day on earth, with a solid commitment and faith in Jesus. By all accounts, including my own, she was a real cut above and righteous woman of God. All of us that knew her miss her dearly and look forward to the day we will see her again – and we will.

I wonder if you can face your life or your death knowing the same? Maybe you have been deceived into thinking that you are basically good enough to make it to heaven. I would remind you that no matter how decent of a human being you are, you are still basically dirt and in desperate need of a savior.

If my friends Leo and Gina were able to speak to you, they would tell you that what they are seeing now is far better than anything they had ever seen on earth. They would tell you that the promises of God, through Jesus Christ, are real and He is worthy to be trusted.

Maybe you have convinced yourself that you are not going to die somehow. Wake up and look over those figures again! Maybe you have been lulled into thinking that this decision is not that important and you can just put it off until later. Your decision to not decide is still in fact a decision.

TO CHOOSE NOT TO CHOOSE IS TO CHOOSE.

Grab hold of Jesus, get on your knees and fight for your life like a man! Jesus is the one thing you've got going for you in this messed up world and you had better take Him seriously.

My friend Leo takes Jesus seriously. He gets it when Paul said that for him to live was Christ and for him to die was gain. That's a fancy King James way of saying that because of his relationship with Jesus, if he lives or if he dies he's a winner either way.

ONE THING I KNOW

2000 years ago a blind man sat outside the temple and happened to be there when Jesus walked by.

At the very end of John chapter 8, the Bible says just before Jesus met the blind man, Jesus Himself made people unable to see Him as they began to pick up stones with the intent of a Rodney King riot. This same Jesus that made the Pharisees unable to see, gave a blind beggar the gift of sight and all on the very same day.

As is always the case when God moves, there was a huge controversy from the skeptics and critics. A trial took place and this man that had been blind, found himself in the hot seat trying to answer the mechanics of exactly how this miracle had happened.

"Tell us how He healed you!"
"How long have you been His disciple?"
"Why would He heal you and not the guy next to you?"
"Were you really blind to begin with?"
"Who do you say Jesus is?"

This uneducated, uncultured, unskilled brother looked at the high and the mighty of his day with his brand new set of eyes and answered the only way he could.

"One thing I know, that, whereas I was blind, now I see."
John 9:25

He was saying, "No sir, I don't have it all figured out, but it doesn't take a rocket scientist to know the difference between light and darkness, life and death, and yes, blindness and sight. We can learn a lot from our brother's response.

There are a lot of things I don't understand. I have a lot of questions concerning the providence of God and the mysteries of His holiness. There are times when I can get caught up in pondering predestination and the choices God commands us to make. There are moments when I look back into the face of someone dealing with tragedy and I don't have an answer for the exact mechanics of how things happen and why. But in the midst of all of that, there is ONE THING I KNOW. I, like our brother 2000 years ago, was blind until Jesus showed up and now I see.

I had thought I would always live in darkness, but Jesus had much better plans for my life than I did. Sometimes you answer the hard questions with the reality of the obvious and that is where you stick.

SOMETHING TO SIP ON:

The Spirit of the Lord is upon me, because he hath anointed me to preach the gospel to the poor; he hath sent me to heal the brokenhearted, to preach deliverance to the captives, and recovering of sight to the blind, to set at liberty them that are bruised,
Luke 4:18

BOOK DEDICATION

I just recently finished writing my 2nd book. It's been a year and half long project that at times has nearly driven me crazy with its challenges. That's ironic when you consider that the subject matter deals with having a right mind in Christ. It's called SOUL INVASION and it is nearly 300 pages of biblical strategies for victorious thinking.

I had to decide about the dedication at the beginning of the chapters. In my last book, "Miracles With A Message", it made perfect sense to publicly thank my bride, Leanna, for the miracle of our 15 year marriage. That is kind of the way I see a book dedication as really more of a very public "thank you".

I could have said thank you to all the people that have done their part to drive me crazy throughout my ministry. Without them, I would have never had to spend untold hours crying out to God, while banging my head on the floor. Without truly seeking God on this subject, I may never have had the truth revealed to me and I would never have had a chance to be free indeed.

Instead, I decided to dedicate this work to the Demoniac of Gadara whose story is told in Mark chapter 5 and Luke chapter 8. I hope that you will go there and read this story for yourself.

I have thought a lot about him over the years and have even stood near the very cliff in Galilee where that famous herd of pigs plunged to their deaths.

They were possessed with the demonic thoughts that had tormented him for years.

Though we don't know his name, sometimes I feel like I know him. Even though none of us have ever heard him speak, his testimony has been preached for 2000 years. I'm a big fan of his because whether he meant to or not, he has helped me personally and encouraged me in the Lord.

I would pay big bucks to see the befuddled look on those faces that saw him just after he had his encounter with Jesus. There he was, no longer hurting himself, no longer ashamed, but in the presence of the King, with a right mind. That's how I want to be.

I finished my dedication to him by saying this:

"Like you, the readers of this book are nameless to me, but I pray that they meet the same Jesus and have the same testimony. I will see you on the Great Day my friend. Your Brother in Christ, Troy."

SOMETHING TO SIP ON:

Out of all the uncanny ways that Jesus can heal someone, I put a high priority on mental healings.

We know that Jesus heals people of disease as far as physical bodies go, but do we really know that Jesus heals us of mental malfunctions as well?

FRIENDS IN LOW PLACES

A long time before Garth Brooks ever ruined that famous "Black Tie Affair", I used to pride myself in the sorry company I kept. I would often brag on it because I was as sorry company as the people I ran around with.

I played football, so I was friends with all the "jocks". I was on the drama team, so I was friends with the "U.I.L. nerds". I was a guitar player, so I was friends with the "head bangers". I dabbled in bull riding, so I was friends with all the "ropers". I smoked things I shouldn't have, so I was friends with all the "freaks". The only click I didn't fit into was the group of really smart kids and that was for obvious reasons.

Yes, I remember the salad days of being surrounded by lots of people that would give me the thumbs up and all the kudos. I remember it, but I have to really stretch my brain to do so. The reason being is, because in 1986 I gave my life to Jesus and the crowds dispersed. People ran from me like a box full of Willard's rats.

For some it was the final straw and bonafied proof of my insanity. For others it was the "I-was-too-religious" thing and over the top. You hear that kind of thing when you go to church more than just on Christmas & Easter. Whatever the reasons, I found myself "un-surrounded" and it didn't take long for that to happen.

Over the years I have experienced this same kind of thing in many different ways, but the truth of the matter is, I don't really look for close friends anymore. Now don't get me wrong, I like having some people in my life that I can laugh and cut up with. I need to let my hair down sometimes with close friends that love me and just want to be my friend. But nonetheless, I have come to the place that I do not need a lot of those kinds of relationships. In fact, I don't think it is really a good thing to have too many close friends. Jesus had twelve people that He kept close to disciple and only three of those were close friends. There is wisdom in that.

Sometimes the people we love the most might be our greatest hindrance. Sometimes we can't be the people God has called us to be and have the same friends we used to have.

A few years ago I was on a missions trip to England and Scotland. While I was there, I had a chance to go to that famous castle in Edinburgh. This was a big kick for me because I am a William Wallace fan (BRAVEHEART) and a collector of Christian books on martyrs. So many unbelievable "Jesus Freaks" were put to the flames on the grounds of that famous stone building. The medieval church rounded up people by the thousands for daring to pray, preach or even read the Bible without their seal of approval. All of them were brutalized, terrorized and executed for loving Jesus more than they loved their own lives. These are my heroes and I stood at that very place that is now a paved over parking lot.

One of the stories that comes from the dungeons of Edinburgh tells of a Bishop that dared to copy the Bible in the common English language, so that the Word of God was accessible to the common people. The medieval Catholic Church called it blasphemy to print the Word in a "vulgar" language, so they brought him in chains before a high court.
After a lengthy interrogation, he was thrown into a dungeon while he waited his turn to be burned alive at the stake.

At some point that night he heard the rattle of chains and the turning of a key. His lifelong friend and fellow priest stepped into that filthy place and they embraced each other with a hug. In that dim lit dungeon cell his friend explained that he had worked a deal with the existing powers and that he was there to reason with him. All he had to do to save his life was sign a public confession that he had sinned and give them his word that he would never preach to commoners again.

"I am your friend," he said, handing him the scroll. "I do not want to see you burn to death." With that, the man of God put his back against the wall and looked sadly to his fellow priest.

"You are indeed the friend of flesh," he said, handing the scroll back to him. "But you are not the friend of my soul."

I thought about that brother when I was in Scotland and I think about him now. Though I never met him, he made an incredible impact in my life. A lot of times the friends of our flesh are not the friends of our souls. Most of the time we will have to choose between those familiar relationships and those strategically planted alliances that God has given us. I thank God for those strategic alliances that are also good friends, but I am not surprised that they are few and far between.

My highest priority in friendship is none other than Jesus Himself. The fact of the matter is that we desire close friends because we are made in the image of God and God desires close friends. Abraham was called the friend of God (2 Chronicles 20:7), and God spoke to Moses "face to face, as a man speaks to his friend" (Ex 33:11).

Are your friends in low places or are you the friend of the Most High of all?

Greater love hath no man than this,
that a man lay down his life for his friends.
Ye are my friends, if ye do whatsoever I command you.
John 15:13 & 14

KNOCK-DOWN DRAG-OUT

A little over a month ago, I had the chance to visit a church in Cuba. It turned out to be an incredible missions trip. On a Sunday night, a pastor was taking Jeff Sherrill and me to visit a church about 50 miles east of Havana. We were riding in a 57 Chevy station wagon when we turned a corner to get on the main highway.

There just ahead of us, a mob of people moved back and forth across the road. We were not sure what it was at first, but a moment later we saw clearly what all the commotion was about. Two men were fighting in hand-to-hand combat; both of them armed with machetes! Both of them wild-eyed, panting and bleeding. Both of them trying to kill the other. Both of them shirtless with numerous wounds on their bodies. It was an amazing thing to see.

Just as we passed them, one threw his blade at the other and barely missed. I could see through the back window that the armed man jumped on top of the other and was hacking away at his head and neck as the crowd encircled them. I don't know if he killed him, but I suspect so. I have seen a lot of fights in my life, but nothing like that. Combat is brutal. War is hell. A fight to the death is without mercy.

When I think of the times I have fought with God, the times I have struggled with Him, the times I have outright gone to war against His will for my life, I see that I have ended up the same way every time. Just like that young man, on my back, defenseless, beat up and surrounded by people that don't give a rip. Yet in every single case, Jesus has shown me mercy.

You shouldn't be surprised when the world doesn't show you mercy. That is the nature of the world, but the nature of God is to pick you up, heal you and call you His friend. If you are having a knock-down-drag-out with God over something, let me encourage you to drop your weapon and submit to your maker. He loves you and doesn't want to see you beat up and bleeding. Nobody can show you mercy the way that He wants to.

SOMETHING TO SIP ON:

But God, who is rich in mercy, for his great love wherewith he loved us, Even when we were dead in sins, hath quickened us together with Christ, (by grace ye are saved;) And hath raised us up together, and made us sit together in heavenly places in Christ Jesus:
Ephesians 2:4-6

And I thank Christ Jesus our Lord, who hath enabled me, for that he counted me faithful, putting me into the ministry; Who was before a blasphemer, and a persecutor, and injurious: but I obtained mercy, because I did it ignorantly in unbelief.
1 Timothy 1:12-13

Blessed are the merciful: for they shall obtain mercy.
Matthew 5:7

HOW QUICK IS YOUR MODEM?

I love the internet. In a strange kind of way, I think it's a lot like Las Vegas. See, Vegas is one of the greatest places in the world a guy can go to if you don't drink and you don't gamble. What, a Jesus Freak that goes to Vegas?! Why not? The flights are cheap, the enormous rooms in those grand hotels are very inexpensive, they've got the best shows and the biggest buffets, the Grand Canyon is awesome. Who wouldn't want to go a place like that?

If you can keep from putting your hard earned money in those stupid machines, for the sake of hearing whistles and watching fruit spin, you can have an awesome time for next to nothing. I have personally beat Vegas several times by simply taking advantage of all the amenities, all the free stuff and not wasting a dime on booze or gambling.

The internet is like that. It's an awesome thing to have in your life as long as you don't stop at the bad parts of town. It can be a tremendous blessing or a terrible curse, depending on your ability to maintain Godly character. For somebody like me that does tons of research, it is an invaluable tool that makes me more effective at preaching the Gospel.

This last year I upgraded to what's called a T1 line. It makes everything so incredibly fast and it's the way the internet is supposed to be. As soon as you click it, the page is there and that's the way it has to be with me. I cannot stand it when things are slow. I'm a fast paced kind of guy and a 14k modem will launch me into a rubber room with a straight jacket.

I have noticed that the church in America tends to run on 14k when we should be way past broadband. What should take 5 months to accomplish, typically takes 25 years and just like the myth of evolution, our change is so slow that nobody ever sees it. The impact that should take place never happens. God help us.

This week's cup of Jehovah java will be sipped by some and gulped by others, depending on how fast you are able to receive things.

Have you ever noticed that some of our churches are filled with the same 25 people that were there 25 years ago? Have you noticed that they sit in the same pew and that they are basically the same people they were 25 years ago? I run from these people the way my youngest boy runs from firecrackers.

Have you seen the guy that gets saved and then is launched into victory at a much higher speed? Within a few months he understands the Bible and is off of drugs, off of booze. His prayer life is advanced. His days are full of peace and joy. He starts winning people for Jesus immediately and it didn't take 25 years. It happened quickly or "SUDDENLY" as the Bible puts it. What do you think the difference is between people who bullet train with God and people who drip like molasses?

I can tell you. It all has to do with how many different levels God is able to deal with you on at one single time. It's a lot like the difference between dial up and satellite speed.

If your relationship with God is so shallow that He can only deal with you on one issue or one part of your life at a time, things will move very slow for you. If you can receive His instruction and His Word on say 15 or 20 issues or parts of your life at one time, then what He is trying to accomplish in your life will move 15 or 20 times faster. Instead of you going though your mess for 15 or 20 years, you can move through in one.

I would suggest that this is for you. Since you do not know how many years you have left, you had better learn how to let God be God in your life and not just one little part of it.

Can you handle being submitted to God on multiple levels all at the same time? Are you growing in Christ on a prayer level at the same time you are growing on multiple other levels? Can God show you how to forgive at the same time He shows you how to be an awesome employee or a wonderful grandparent? Can God correct you about laziness at the same time He encourages you for not being ugly to that crazy lady in Wal-Mart? If you can handle a broadband of data from the Lord at one time, then the pages of the seasons of your life will come and go at a much faster pace.

Judge yourself on how many levels God can deal with you on at a single time and ask yourself, "How quick is my modem?"

PASS THE SALT

One of the greatest natural wonders that this planet has to offer is a place we call the Dead Sea.

Because of the rapid evaporation of that desert place (about 5 feet per year) the water leaves behind incredible amounts of salts and sulfates that are mined and sent all over the world. The thing about the Dead Sea is that it is the lowest place on the face of the planet. This tear shaped wonder is more than 1,200 feet below sea level and the salt is so thick, not a single fish lives in it. People come from all over the world to "sit" in the thick water because you can't sink.

God made it this way and strategically placed it in Israel for all the world to get the spiritual illustration in the geographical picture. Because of its low place, it is only able to receive from rivers and never able to contribute to any other. It has no outgoing sources, only incoming sources.

Like a lot of people, though it is full of riches, it has no life in it. It is only able to receive and never able to give.

God has called all of us to be givers. I'm not just talking about money. I am talking about our very lives.

He that findeth his life shall lose it: and he that loseth his life
for my sake shall find it.
Matt 10:39

This is the principle. A mom is an awesome mom (like my mom was) because she gives her life away. Instead of everything being about her, she becomes the taxi service, laundromat, football cheerleader, sex-ed counselor, chef extraordinaire, financial genius and all the countless other things that she must become in order to give her children life.

It's not that it is convenient or easy for her, it is just that she chooses to give, instead of constantly receive. I thank God for the fewer and fewer who choose to be Galilee instead of the Dead Sea.

More and more of us today look at our time, our assets, our treasure, our talents, our opinions, our expression, our example, our experience, and our knowledge that has come into our lives and we count them much too valuable to give away.

While constant and consistent is that flow into our lives, we count it only as far as how rich it makes us personally and how we estimate our own self value and worth. Very little trickles out. Just like the Dead Sea, though we are full of riches, we are not full of life. Our life fills full of sorrow and looks like a tear and ultimately our place is the lowest region of the earth.

Refuse to be dead! Refuse the impulse to horde and hang onto you and all that you have. Be a giver and give your life to God! Give your life to Jesus and to His purpose and plan. Give, give, give and determine that the things that have come into your life might not be about you at all. Maybe there is something a whole lot bigger than us going on here. Maybe we actually don't own anything, but we are actually only tested as stewards.

Be a faithful giver of whatever valuable thing the Lord has trusted you with.

Never be afraid to pass the salt.

SOMETHING TO SIP ON:

In ancient times, the Dead Sea looked like a tear. In contrast, the shape of the Sea of Galilee looked like a harp. The contrast between the two could not be more apparent, since a harp represents praise.

It's kind of sad to me that 2 bodies of water could be in the same geographical location, connected to the same exact river and yet be at opposite ends of the pole.

You find people like that in families, churches and in generations. The same water is offered to both, yet one is teaming with life and the other is polluted with the poisons of this world.   Paul made mention of this mystery in 2 Corinthians 2:15-16 NKJV:

For we are to God the fragrance of Christ among those who are being saved and among those who are perishing. To the one we are the aroma of death leading to death, and to the other the aroma of life leading to life.

HITTING THE NAIL ON THE HEAD

As a Pastor, I get scared to answer the phone sometimes. You never know what might be on the other end. Monday, a visiting Pastor from Uganda answered the phone for me because I had gone to town. On the other end was a good friend of mine that I have known since we were little kids, a man by the name of Mike Duke.

Mike was very upset and on the verge of a total melt down. He was asking for prayer as he and his wife were speeding towards the Hospital.

"What's the matter?" Pastor Patrick asked. Mike's reply sent a chill through the phone. "I HAVE SHOT MY WIFE IN THE HEAD WITH A NAIL GUN!"

Suzanne and Mike work together building fences and in a freak accident, he had slipped and accidentally hit her right between the eyes with a 120 pound air driven nail gun. Suzanne was conscience but bleeding very badly and not very happy about the prospect of what that nail was doing to her brain. Pastor

Patrick prayed, and into the emergency room they went. Suzanne explained that other than the obvious hole in her forehead, there was a nail inside her skull somewhere. ....BUT GOD.

After a few minutes of pandemonium, X-rays revealed that there was no nail at all inside her head. To everyone's amazement and for no natural reason whatsoever, the nail had ricocheted and bounced right off her skull! Later that afternoon they would find the nail at the jobsite. They brought it to church on Wednesday. It was a tremendous miracle.

Not only does this confirm to Mike that his wife is the hardest headed woman in Johnson County, it confirms to Suzanne that God protects her even in the midst of her husband's malfunctions.

We serve a mighty and powerful God. There was no need for Suzanne to take a nail when Jesus had taken three for all of us.

SOMETHING TO SIP ON:

He that dwelleth in the secret place of the most High shall abide under the shadow of the Almighty.
I will say of the LORD, He is my refuge and my fortress: my God; in him will I trust.
Surely he shall deliver thee from the snare of the fowler, and from the noisome pestilence.
He shall cover thee with his feathers, and under his wings shalt thou trust: his truth shall be thy shield and buckler.
Thou shalt not be afraid for the terror by night; nor for the arrow that flieth by day;
Nor for the pestilence that walketh in darkness; nor for the destruction that wasteth at noonday.
A thousand shall fall at thy side, and ten thousand at thy right hand; but it shall not come nigh thee.

Only with thine eyes shalt thou behold
and see the reward of the wicked.
Because thou hast made the LORD, which is my refuge,
even the most High, thy habitation;
There shall no evil befall thee,
neither shall any plague come nigh thy dwelling.
For he shall give his angels charge over thee,
to keep thee in all thy ways.
They shall bear thee up in their hands,
lest thou dash thy foot against a stone.
Thou shalt tread upon the lion and adder: the young lion and
the dragon shalt thou trample under feet.
Because he hath set his love upon me, therefore will I deliver
him: I will set him on high, because he hath known my name.
He shall call upon me, and I will answer him: I will be with
him in trouble; I will deliver him, and honour him.
With long life will I satisfy him, and shew him my salvation.
Psalms 91: 1-16

BATTLE MOUTH

Right now at this very moment there is a tremendous battle raging and casualties are extremely high. You will not hear about this war on CNN, but it is just as real as any overseas. You do not have to be in Iraq or Afghanistan, this war can take place while you drive to work or sit at your kitchen table. These battles are fought in your mind, in your heart and in the unseen. If you loose this war, you loose absolutely everything.

I want to take you to boot camp several thousand years ago. General Jehovah explains exactly how to win in an "un-winnable" battle.

In Deuteronomy chapter 20, he starts off by saying, ***"When thou goest out to battle against thine enemies, and seest horses, and chariots, and a people more than thou, be not afraid of them: for the LORD thy God is with thee, which brought thee up out of the land of Egypt."***

Every day you and I are fighting battles against insurmountable odds. We constantly find ourselves out of the shallow and into the deep end, in the things that are against us. I feel out of my league all the time, in some of the struggles I face and so do you. That is the nature of the day we live in. We walk through our days the way Afghan families walk through mine fields, very carefully, with the knowledge that anything could blow up at any moment.

God said, when you see that the things that are against you are bigger than you, first of all steady yourself in the understanding that you are not alone, but that God Himself is with us. The second instruction He gives us is a little off the wall. He doesn't give us specific instructions as what to do; He gives us specific instructions as what to say.

Before anyone was lead into battle, there were certain right things that had to be verbalized. The first thing that had to be controlled to win that battle was not the enemy, but the mouth of the person being attacked.

Let me talk to you about your battle mouth. One of the most important strategies God gives us for overcoming anything, even our own minds, is learning the discipline of speaking right words. I know that people have been extreme in this area and a lot of junk has been taught, but don't throw the baby out with the bath water. You let God get ahold of your mouth and your life will change. As Bill Murray once said, "That's the fact, Jack."

Another fact is that we don't know how to speak right words automatically. The impulse to speak is always carnal in nature and filthy in substance. Just like any other part of our walk with the Lord, we have to be taught. If we are going to be taught by the Lord we first have to be teachable people. When you are real with God about your mouth, He will be real with you. In fact, if you will put your ear to the air concerning this subject, He will "teach you what thou shalt say." (Exodus 4:10-12)

Do you have a constant conflict going on between your ears? Maybe it is time to bury your mental hatchet and make friends with your memories. Quit talking about the mess that happened 20 years ago and tell folks what you are thankful for.

A soft answer turneth away wrath: but grievous words stir up anger.
Proverbs 15:1

A lot of the time we attract or repel wrath by the words we speak .When you always have something ugly to say, you're going to attract the dislike or the wrath of others. Just like that, your mouth, when not under control of the Holy Spirit, makes your mind a mental magnet for strife, trouble and conflict.

I am going to throw out some verses that may be familiar to you. Don't just look at these principles as far as what they do naturally and spiritually. See that they do the same in the mental arena as well.

Right words will breathe energy and life into everything around you, including your own thinking habits.

A whole tongue is a tree of Life.
Proverbs 15:4

Right words, at the right time, can change everything.

A man hath Joy by the answer of his mouth and a word spoken in due season how sweet it is.
Proverbs 15:23

Right words can dictate what dreams live and what dreams die.

Death and life are in the power of a tongue.
And they that love it shall eat the fruit there of.
Proverbs 18:21

If you are speaking His Word, you are speaking life, if not, you are speaking death.

Right words can get you out of big-time trouble.

> *But the mouth of the upright will deliver them..*
> **Proverbs 12:6**

Right words can bring healing to all kinds of arenas.

> *The tongue of the wise is health.*
> **Proverbs 12:18**

Jesus wants in on every part of your life. He wants you to prosper, but by His rules. The bottom line is, that there is no way you cannot prosper if you let God get ahold of how you speak and what you say. So what are you waiting for? Make a new commitment to God to be teachable in this area of your life.

Right now might be a great time to repent for producing a septic line instead of a sword from our mouths. Get on your knees, fight like a man and give your mouth to Jesus Christ. He is the one that made it. It ought to belong to Him anyway.

THE ESSENCE OF EVIL

I was in a hotel room near Tulsa, OK after taking our youth to camp last week. For several hours Leanna and I had a rare opportunity to hang out on the couch and just "veg". Now being a typical guy, I began to wear the remote out trying to view all 100 channels at the same time. After my 3rd or 4th time around the horn, I landed on a documentary about the famous Nazi trials that followed the 2nd World War. I decided to pitch my tent on that channel and dig in.

A writer had taken the opportunity to follow all of the trials as close as he could and really hone in on what made those guys tick. He watched meticulously, took notes, looked up their backgrounds, listened to their defense and personally interviewed many of them, all in an attempt to find out what could cause just smart people to do such heinous crimes against humanity.

When it was all said and done, he believed he had the answer. All of the men tried had different backgrounds, different educations, different religious beliefs, different careers, they came from different parts of the country and were all different in age. There was one common thread though that ran between all of them and kept them close in the Nazi affiliation. The same thing that made it OK for the chemist to make his gas, was the same thing that made it OK for the doctor to experiment skin grafts on live little boys.

"THE LACK OF EMPATHY"

There was not anything inside any of those men that enabled them to find pity on anybody. They could not feel the pain of anyone other than themselves. In the words of Pink Floyd, "they had all become comfortably numb".

We need to make sure that we are not like that. When our heart is tapped into the heart of God, we see things that others don't see and feel things that others don't feel. According to the book of Jude, the way we make a difference is by having compassion. It is our ability and our willingness to get in somebody else's mess, that shows Jesus to this generation. I encourage you to deal with the Nazi part of your heart and make yourself be willing to be touched by the lives of those around you.

For we have not an high priest which cannot
be touched with the feeling of our infirmities; but was in all
points tempted like as we are, yet without sin.
Hebrews 4:15

CAN THESE BONES LIVE?

In Ezekiel 37 there is the famous story when the Spirit put the prophet in the midst of a graveyard and asked him a serious question. "Son of man, can these bones live?"

I love it when God asks a question. He doesn't ask because He does not know the answer, He asks because we do not know the answer, and until we know the truth, we cannot be set free.

Adam, where are you? Saul, why do you persecute me? Jonah, do you do well to be so angry? Cain, if you do well, shall you not be accepted? There are a myriad of questions throughout the Bible intended to bring us to the truth. But this is one question I know that Ezekiel wanted to get right. You see, when you're standing in the midst of an untold number of dead bodies and God asks you a question, one could conclude that the bodies around you are those who couldn't answer correctly before you. You talk about pressure to get something right!

Ezekiel was no dummy, so he comes up with a BRILLIANT answer. He says, "YOU know Lord."

Sometimes when we are overwhelmed in the midst of things we don't understand, the smartest thing we can do at the time, is to just concede to the fact that God does understand, even though we do not.

SOMETHING TO SIP ON:

For Christ sent me not to baptize, but to preach the gospel:
not with wisdom of words,
lest the cross of Christ should be made of none effect.
For the preaching of the cross is to them that perish
foolishness; but unto us which are saved it is the power of God.
For it is written, I will destroy the wisdom of the wise, and will
bring to nothing the understanding of the prudent.
Where is the wise? Where is the scribe?
Where is the disputer of this world?
Hath not God made foolish the wisdom of this world?
For after that in the wisdom of God the world by wisdom knew
not God, it pleased God by the foolishness
of preaching to save them that believe.
For the Jews require a sign, and the Greeks seek after wisdom:
But we preach Christ crucified, unto the Jews a stumbling
block, and unto the Greeks foolishness;
But unto them which are called, both Jews and Greeks, Christ
the power of God, and the wisdom of God.
Because the foolishness of God is wiser than men; and the
weakness of God is stronger than men.
1 Cor 1:17-25

TO HELL WITH HALLOWEEN

Every year at the end of October, our little church puts on a giant Fallfest, as an outreach. We lovingly call it "To Hell With Halloween".

I would like to think that I am one of the most nonreligious pastors around, but with that said, I also will stick with Jesus if it appears to be religious. There are just some things that a Christian should not be a part of, and for me and my house, Halloween is definitely one of those things.

There are some things I refuse to celebrate and certain things I will never be a part of, even if it is the culture I live in. I mean gee-whiz, I can honestly tell you that you will never see me lifting my shirt for beads at the annual party on bourbon street. Jesus Freaks don't do that. Nor will you see me dressing my family up like the devil and chanting the same mantra that the druids used to chant; "trick or treat". I know that it is accepted in our culture, but it causes my "cringe meter" to tap out when I think about it. It is not accepted in the Kingdom of Heaven so I say to Hell with Halloween.

About three years ago, I was doing some research and I found something worth celebrating on October 31st. This is not a day when the church should be celebrating all things evil with the world, but it should be celebrated as the day Martin Luther gave the devil a fat lip and black eye.

On October 31, 1517 Martin Luther posted his 95 Theses in Wittenberg. By God's grace, Luther's courageous act of challenging the corruption and unbiblical practices of the Medieval Catholic hierarchy launched the Great Reformation. This was something that had to be done, and God raised up the perfect man for the job. Look at what this brother said when asked to give an explanation for his "insolence and rebellion".

"Unless I am convinced by Scripture or clear reasoning that I am in error - for popes and councils have often erred and contradicted themselves - I cannot recant, for I am subject to the Scriptures I have quoted; my conscience is captive to the Word of God. It is unsafe and dangerous to do anything against one's conscience. Here I stand. I cannot do otherwise. So help me God. Amen."- *Martin Luther*

Here are just a few of the incredible blessings that came to believers as a result the Reformation that brother Martin kicked off that day:

- The Bible available in our own language.
- Scripture alone is our final authority.
- Justification is received by faith alone.
- Christ alone is the head of the Church.
- Religious freedom.
- Liberty of conscience.
- Free enterprise.
- Lex Rex (the rule of law).
- Separation of powers.

- Constitutionally limited republics.
- The Lordship of Christ in all areas of life.

Now you might take these truths for granted, but these were principles & privileges that Christians were not allowed to know, study or practice until Martin Luther made a stand on Oct 31st in 1517.

The spark was only started there and the Holy Roman church did it's best to extinguish the fire that followed with the blood of untold numbers of Christian martyrs. These "heretics" suffered horrible torture and death for "blasphemous" charges such as:

- Daring to preach the Gospel to the poor without permission from Rome.

- Daring to translate, read or write the scriptures into "vulgar" languages such as were common to people that needed the Word. (Like English in England or French in France)

- Daring to believe or teach that Jesus Christ and not Mary or a priest or a saint or the Pope is the mediator between God and Man. Can you imagine the audacity of a Christian wanting to put their trust in Christ? That was a capital offense and the Catholics would torture you until you "confessed your sin" and then they would send you to heaven by publicly burning you alive. What a wonderful ministry they had!

This is just barely scratching the surface of how dark the Dark Ages really were, but the light began to come on in the darkest day of the year. It was on October 31st that Martin Luther nailed his 95 points to the front doors of the church in Wittenberg. It was from that day forward that people began to have the courage to stand up against the seemingly unstoppable menace the Church of Rome really was.

Martin Luther's courage caused others to have courage. The truth of the life that is in Christ and Christ alone began to get spread once again.

"If I profess with the loudest voice and clearest exposition every portion of the truth of God except precisely that point which the world and the devil are at that moment attacking, then I am not confessing Christ, however boldly I may be professing Him. Where the battle rages, there the loyalty of the soldier is proved; and to be steady on all the battlefront besides is merely flight and disgrace if he flinches at that point." - Martin Luther

So instead of celebrating death and Hell on the 31st, you might ought to celebrate the liberty in Christ that we live, and the countless miracles God has had to do, to pull off the walk we have with him, free from the tyrannical whims of somebody else. I encourage you to join me in saying glory be to the Lord Jesus Christ and to Hell with Halloween.

BRAIN FREEZE

In the hot summer sun of Texas, it is easy to eat an ice cream in a hurry or drink something cold too fast. If you make that mistake, you get an instant migraine headache that you won't soon forget.

A few years ago, I was in a 7-Eleven with a missionary from East Africa. He looked over at a SLURPY advertisement and asked, "What is a brain freeze?" I said, "Here let me show ya." I handed him a cold, cherry Slurpy, put a giant straw in it and said, "Drink this as fast as you can for about 15 seconds."

About 20 seconds later he dropped the drink on the floor and stumbled out into the parking lot with both hands on his forehead. He didn't think it was funny, but I and the guy behind the counter got a really big kick out of it. A few minutes later he came back in smiling and helped us clean up the mess. It was a hoot!

Spiritually speaking, it is very important for Christians to learn the God-given art of stopping thoughts before they turn into something else. I call that a "brain freeze." You might not be able to control your feelings, but you can learn how to control your thoughts.

It is your thoughts that control your feelings and it is your feelings, that many times, affects your actions. Serving God in your thinking produces victory all throughout your life.

My second book, "SOUL INVASION", deals extensively with how to effectively learn the art of "brain freeze". Not that I have obtained anything, but God has really given me some sure fire ways to have true, every day victory in our gray matter.

See, thoughts will always progress into something else, so we have got to learn how to let the Holy Spirit invade our thinking. Stop what you're doing and ask Jesus to you teach the art of "spiritual brain freeze".

SOMETHING TO SIP ON:

"Commit thy works unto the Lord and
thy thoughts shall be established."
Proverbs 16:3

A double minded man is unstable in all his ways.
James 1:8

Young men likewise exhort to be sober minded.
In all things shewing thyself a pattern of good works:
Titus 2:6-7

For they that are after the flesh do mind the things of the flesh;
but they that are after the Spirit the things of the Spirit.
For to be carnally minded is death;
but to be spiritually minded is life and peace.
Because the carnal mind is enmity against God: for it is not
subject to the law of God, neither indeed can be.
Rom 8:5-7

THE BIG FISH

You might not know it, but our national "ally" Saudi Arabia, is one of the world's worst offenders of atrocities against your brothers and sisters in Christ. I am not trying to be controversial, but it is a fact that while we pander to them, protect them and send them billions, they torture and murder Christians without being held accountable. Many of them simply for owning a Bible. You did know that it is a capital offense to own a Bible in Saudi Arabia or did CNN fail to mention that?

A law was passed several years ago that was sanctioned by the United Nations and then quickly swept under the rug. The law states that it is a capital offense to try to convert anyone to Christianity on the grounds of an Islamic mosque.

Now that might not seem so extreme. What is outrageous and not publicized is that Muslim countries declare the borders of their nations to be a mosque, so that makes it illegal to spread the gospel or own anything Christian within those borders.

In the early 1990's, the most wanted man to the Saudi government's secret police was not a terrorist or a murderer but a pastor that dared to "print" tracts with Bible verses. He had the audacity to give people the good news of Jesus Christ in a country controlled by Muslims. Something that is never permitted in a country controlled by Muslims and this of all places the home of Mecca.

The day they tore down his front door, assaulted his wife and children, and arrested all of them is a day that Pastor Wally Magdangal will never forget. Sitting in the back seat of a secret policeman's car, about to be taken off and tortured, the officer in the front seat turned around smiling.

"I have finally caught the big fish," he gloated through yellow teeth.

"No," Pastor Wally replied "You have only caught a little fisherman."

He was put into prison by the religious authorities in Riyadh, Saudi Arabia on October 14, 1992. He was humiliated and severely tortured. For his crime, the high court of Saudi Arabia sentenced him to death by public hanging on December 25, 1992.

But through a series of miracles, God moved His hands to spare him from the death penalty. He did this by using his wife and daughter, and Christians, human rights organizations and some politically influential people from all over the world to protest his death sentence and appeal for his freedom to the Monarchy of Saudi Arabia.

He was released the night before the scheduled date of execution and celebrated Christmas Eve on board an aircraft that flew him to freedom. His co-pastors and staff that were indigenous to Saudi Arabia were not allowed to go free and some were executed.

SOMETHING TO SIP ON:

For more information go to your web browser and type in Christian persecution Saudi Arabia and see what comes up. Or just go to this site www.persecution.org/Countries/saudi_arabia.

There is a ministry called Open Doors based out of Santa Ana, California, which monitors the persecution of Christians across the world. They issue a "Hall of Shame" every six months. Their mid-2000 report lists the following:

"Saudi Arabia as the world's worst persecutor of Christians. Despite the fact that there are 600,000 ex-patriate Christians living there, Saudi Arabia still has the unsavory title of the world's worst persecutor of Christians. The kingdom does not permit any practice of the Christian faith."

In March 1997, Filipino Christian Donato Lama was deported after being subjected to 17 months in prison and 70 lashes. He was arrested when police discovered a photo album snapshot of him leading a Catholic communion service in a private home.

"Freedom of religion does not exist," the U.S. State Department's 1997 Human Rights Report on Saudi Arabia states. "Islam is the official religion, and all citizens must be Muslims. The government prohibits the public (or private) practice of other religions." *Source Flash news by Barbara Baker*

HOUND ON YOUR TRAIL

Awhile back, the sequel to a big hit from the summer before opened to tons of teenage moviegoers called "Final Destination". It's a story about several friends who cheat death by not dying when they were supposed to, and for the whole two hours, death is out to get them. One by one, death hunts them down and has it's horrible due as they find out they can run, but they can't hide when death is on your trail.

Teenagers tend to have a strange fascination with the hopelessness of death, the same way nearly anybody likes to look down into a bottomless pit. You just can't help but blink into that darkness and say "wow".

I know how to burst the bubble of death's dark side and turn that 2-hour movie into a five-minute dud. All that is needed when people fear that death is after them is, for someone who knows the Truth to speak it.

"DEATH IS NOT AFTER YOU, DEATH ALREADY HAS YOU! Death caught up with you before you were even born."

Wherefore, as by one man sin entered into the world, and death
by sin; and so death passed upon all men,
for that all have sinned.
Romans 5:12

No sir, it is not death that is after you and wants you. Death already has you. It is LIFE that is chasing you down and trying to wrap his arms around you. It is LIFE that wants his way with you and is willing to follow after you no matter where you go. LIFE has a name. JESUS.

C.S. Lewis called Jesus "The Hound of Heaven", meaning that He is the God that pursues. I hope that the day will come when every person who reads this will stop trying to dodge life and let Jesus catch up with them. There's a Hound on your trail and its not the Grim Reaper, it's the blessed Hope. He is the Way, the Truth and yes, He is the LIFE.

SOMETHING TO SIP ON:

For the Son of man is come to save that which was lost.
How think ye? If a man have an hundred sheep, and one of
them be gone astray, doth he not leave the ninety and nine,
and goeth into the mountains, and seeketh that which is gone
astray? And if so be that he find it, verily I say unto you, he
rejoiceth more of that sheep, than of the ninety and nine which
went not astray. Even so it is not the will of your Father which
is in heaven, that one of these little ones should perish.
Matt 18:11-14

LET GO OF THE ROPE

Everybody knows how hard a battle it is with the war between our two ears. Sometimes thoughts we don't want to think, and memories we don't want to remember, will pop back up and scream for our attention.

A famous Jesus person and survivor of the Holocaust named Corrie ten Boom told of not being able to forget a wrong that had been done to her.

She had forgiven the person, but she kept rehashing the incident and so couldn't sleep. Finally Corrie cried out to God for help in putting the problem to rest.

"His help came in the form of a kindly Lutheran pastor," Corrie wrote, "to whom I confessed my failure after two sleepless weeks."

"Up in the church tower," he said, nodding out the window, "is a bell which is rung by pulling on a rope. But you know what? After the sexton lets go of the rope, the bell keeps on swinging. First ding, then dong. Slower and slower until there's a final dong and it stops. I believe the same thing is true of forgiveness. When we forgive, we take our hand off the rope. But if we've been tugging at our grievances for a long time, we mustn't be surprised if the old angry thoughts keep coming for a while. They're just the ding-dongs of the old bell slowing down."

"And so it proved to be. There were a few more midnight reverberations, a couple of dings when the subject came up in my conversations, but the force -- which was my willingness in the matter -- had gone out of them. They came less and less often and at the last stopped altogether: we can trust God not only above our emotions, but also above our thoughts," she said.

SOMETHING TO SIP ON:

Ye have heard that it hath been said, Thou shalt love thy neighbour, and hate thine enemy.
But I say unto you, Love your enemies, bless them that curse you, do good to them that hate you, and pray for them which despitefully use you, and persecute you;
That ye may be the children of your Father which is in heaven: for he maketh his sun to rise on the evil and on the good, and sendeth rain on the just and on the unjust.
For if ye love them which love you, what reward have ye? do not even the publicans the same?
And if ye salute your brethren only, what do ye more than others? do not even the publicans so?
Be ye therefore perfect, even as your Father which is in heaven is perfect.
Matt 5:43-48

COUNTERFEITS

A good friend of mine and the head deacon of our church, works for the Tarrant County District Attorney. He's a really neat guy with a notable name. His first name is Elvis.

A few weeks ago, he handed me a torn piece of a $20 bill and said " Check this out".

It was a remarkable counterfeit. With today's computers and printers, the average Joe can distribute something that, just a few years ago, criminals only dreamed of.

It reminded me of something from the Vietnam War. When the U.S. could not get the nation of Laos to stop taking payoffs from the communists for safe passage through their country, the CIA came up with a plan to wreck the economy in a single day.

They flew over that nation's capital and dumped trillions of counterfeit dollars out of the back of a C-130 and made everybody an instant millionaire. Within 24 hours the dollar of Laos was worth nothing because no one could tell the difference between the counterfeit and the real thing.

That same kind of thing has happened to a lot of Christians all over the world.

The Bible warns us against the dangers of hanging onto spiritual counterfeits:

FALSE WORSHIP (Matthew 15:8-9)
FALSE CHRISTIANS (Galatians 2:3-4)
FALSE APOSTLES (2 Corinthians 11:13)
FALSE DOCTRINES (Hebrews 13:9)
FALSE PRAYER (James 4:3)
FALSE SCIENCE (1 Timothy 6:20)
FALSE CHRISTS (Matthew 24:4-5, 24)

In this day and age, it is super important that God's people be able to tell the difference between what is from the enemy and what is the genuine article.

I pray that you and I will never accept any substitute for the real thing. We don't have to when the genuine article is so available to us.

SOMETHING TO SIP ON:

Then if any man shall say unto you,
Lo, here is Christ, or there; believe it not.
For there shall arise false Christs, and false prophets, and
shall shew great signs and wonders; insomuch that, if it were
possible, they shall deceive the very elect.
Matt 24:23-24 KJV

THE EMPEROR'S NEW SUIT

Way back in 1837 Hans Christian Anderson rocked everybody's world with a parable he called, "The Emperor's New Suit". Here is a short version of it. See if this sounds familiar to you.

Many years ago there lived an emperor who loved beautiful new clothes so much, that he spent all his money on being finely dressed. Indeed, where it was said of other kings that they were at court, it could only be said of him that he was in his dressing room!

One day two swindlers came to the emperor's city. They said that they were weavers, claiming that they knew how to make the finest cloth imaginable. This extraordinary material had the amazing property that, it was to be invisible to anyone who was incompetent or stupid.

"It would be wonderful to have clothes made from that cloth," thought the emperor. So he immediately gave the two swindlers a great sum of money to weave their cloth for him.

They set up their looms and pretended to go to work, although there was nothing at all on the looms. They asked for the finest silk and the purest gold, all of which they hid away, continuing to work on the empty looms, often late into the night.

"I would really like to know how they are coming with the cloth!" thought the emperor, but he was a bit uneasy when he recalled that anyone who was unfit for his position or stupid would not be able to see the material. He decided to send someone else to see how the work was progressing.

"I'll send my honest old minister to the weavers," thought the emperor. He's the best one to see how the material is coming. So the good old minister went into the hall where the two swindlers sat working at their empty looms. "Goodness!" thought the old minister, opening his eyes wide. "I cannot see a thing!" But he did not say so.

The emperor sent other officials as well to observe the weavers' progress. They too were startled when they saw nothing, and they too reported back to him how wonderful the material was, advising him to have it made into clothes that he could wear in a grand procession. The entire city was alive in praise of the cloth. "Magnifique! Excellent!" they said, in all languages.

The swindlers stayed up the entire night before the procession was to take place, burning more than sixteen candles. They pretended to take the material from the looms. They cut in the air with large scissors. They sewed with needles but without any thread. Finally they announced, "Behold! The clothes are finished!"

The emperor came to them with his most distinguished cavaliers. The two swindlers raised their arms as though they were holding something and said, "Just look at this suit!" "Yes," said the cavaliers, but they couldn't see a thing, for nothing was there.

The emperor took off all his clothes, and the swindlers pretended to dress him, piece by piece, with the new ones that were to be fitted. They took hold of his waist and pretended to tie something about him. Then the emperor turned and looked into the mirror. "Goodness, they suit you well! What a wonderful fit!" they all said. "What a pattern!"

"Yes, I am ready!" said the emperor. "Don't they fit well?" He turned once again toward the mirror, because it had to appear as though he were admiring himself in all his glory.

The emperor walked beneath the beautiful canopy in the procession, and all the people in the street and in their windows said, "Goodness, the emperor's new clothes are incomparable! What a perfect fit!" No one wanted it to be noticed that he could see nothing, for then it would be said that he was unfit for his position or that he was stupid.

"But he doesn't have anything on!" said a small child. And to that the crowd began to chant "he doesn't have anything on!" The emperor shuddered, for he knew that they were right, but he thought, "The procession must go on!" He carried himself even more proudly, and the chamberlains walked along behind carrying the train that wasn't there. THE END

I really wish it was the end, but let me tell you that the Emperor still walks naked today and the crowds continue to go with it. We are surrounded by general agreements of things that are ridiculous and obviously not the truth, but many with child like faith are afraid to say anything because we will be perceived as stupid!

There are some of us trouble makers that really don't give a rip if our objections to the lies of this generation make us look unintelligent. Try and cram us on a little yellow bus if you like, but we are not the ones walking around naked and pretending to be clothed.

We refuse to go along with the crowd and say that joy is found in alcohol and peace is found in marijuana. We refuse to agree that love is found in promiscuous lifestyles. We object to the general notion that man was not created, but developed from apes. We refuse to agree that homosexual marriage is a beautiful thing. We do not concur with your assumption that the world is not in desperate need of a savior or that people are basically good and will make it to heaven because they paid or did not pay their taxes.

We scream back at the crowd. "It's a lie! It is not true and we will not go along with your false pretence for the sake of looking smart, like you think you look smart!"

When you and I grabbed onto Jesus, we entered the very narrow path that few will walk down, but we entered into something that was true & something very real.

Jesus is the WAY, the TRUTH and the LIFE even when He is called stupid by those walking around naked.

SOMETHING TO SIP ON:

*But he that sinneth against me wrongeth his own soul: all they
that hate me love death.*
Proverbs 8:36

*For the preaching of the cross is to them that perish foolishness;
but unto us which are saved it is the power of God.
For it is written, I will destroy the wisdom of the wise,
and will bring to nothing the understanding of the prudent.
Where is the wise? where is the scribe?
Where is the disputer of this world?
Hath not God made foolish the wisdom of this world?
For after that in the wisdom of God the world by wisdom knew
not God, it pleased God by the foolishness
of preaching to save them that believe.
For the Jews require a sign, and the Greeks seek after wisdom:
But we preach Christ crucified, unto the Jews a stumblingblock,
and unto the Greeks foolishness;
But unto them which are called, both Jews and Greeks,
Christ the power of God, and the wisdom of God.
Because the foolishness of God is wiser than men; and the
weakness of God is stronger than men.*
1 Corinthians 1:18-25

GOOD TO THE LAST DROP

In closing, I would very much like to thank Kayla Smith, Lowell Brown, Mike Thronberry, Dale Gosser & Angela Jordan of the Cleburne Times Review for your hard work and for making "Fresh From The Brewer" available as a column for the good people of Johnson County, Texas.

Kayla, I especially want to thank you for who you are and the difference you make. Your professionalism and your attitude are a witness and testimony. May God bless the work of your hands!

A great big thank you goes out to the people who have supported our ministry this year and made this book possible.

I thank God for my wife and my kids. I love you so much and I am so proud of all of you.

ONE MORE THING TO SIP ON:

Jesus asks, Are ye able to drink of the cup that I shall drink of, and to be baptized with the baptism that I am baptized with?
Matt 20:22

About the author:

Troy Brewer drinks coffee and loves Jesus in Johnson County, Texas. A life long resident of the Joshua area, his church continues to love him in spite of what he did there before he was saved.

He & his wife Leanna, Pastor Open Door Ministries, an outreach church that gives away huge amounts of food to poor families and struggling people. They also head up Answer International, a missions ministry and S.P.A.R.K. International, an outreach that builds and supports orphanages throughout the world.

His music has reached untold numbers throughout the world and to date he has 5 CD's to his credit.

Troy is also author of "Miracles With A Message" and "Soul Invasion".

He is also a noted drawer of musclemen and cars with 50 engines. He has 4 kids, Maegan, Benjamin, Luke & Rhema. They generally get along, even on mornings before he has his first cup.

He can be contacted at:
P.O. Box 1349 Joshua, TX 76058
817-297-6911
www.troybrewer.org
www.opendoorministries.org
freshfromthebrewer@opendoorministries.org

Please let us know if this book has blessed you.

LaVergne, TN USA
30 August 2009
156393LV00002B/7/A ·